# Inspired Life
## Journal

Live an inspired life through gratitude and conscious intention

This journal belongs to:

....................................................

From:  /  / 20          To:  /  / 20

Helene Kempe & David Nolan

**Optimum**Thinking.net

ISBN: 978-0-646-90191-6

## ACKNOWLEDGEMENTS

We would like to acknowledge that this journal has been inspired by ideas from the many personal development leaders whose work we have studied.

Graphic design and layout by Kimberly Cook and Kierrah Jill M. Tanglao

# Contents

Through the challenge of transformation, the butterfly gains the strength and direction to fly.

# Introduction

This journal has been designed to help you consciously create the life that you really want. The clearer you are about what you want, the more easily you will create it. The frustration you feel about what you haven't yet achieved is always directly in proportion to the lack of detail you include in your planning.

There is only one person who gets up in the morning and dedicates their life to living your best life — make everyday count!

The journal provides you the structure to plan at a high level annually, monthly and daily. It is easy to follow and once you make it a habit to use your journal daily, you will start to see amazing progress towards your highest life priorities. As you become more aware daily of what you value and how you spend your resources of time, money, energy and thought, you will be able to direct your focus on what you most want to achieve. When you leave time unplanned, it is quickly filled with other people's priorities. The more you consciously choose how to use your resources to achieve your highest priorities, the more fulfilled your life becomes. Once you complete your planning at this higher level, transfer your Life Priorities to your daily planning.

To make the most of this journal follow these simple steps:

1. Read the introduction and instructions for each section.

2. Then schedule time to complete your:
   ☐ Inspired Life Scope
   ☐ Inspired Life Masterpiece
   ☐ 12 Month Intention Plan

3. Put dates in the Annual Calendar for all of the important events in the year to come.

4. Then schedule some time to do your first Monthly Intention Plan.

5. At the end of each day allocate time in your evening routine to complete the Daily Gratitude and Intention page — you only need 10 mins a day to make an amazing difference to your life.

Listen to your heart and ask yourself what you would really **love to be, to do and to have** in your life.

# Inspired Life Scope

To empower your life it is essential to get clear on what is really important to **you** in your life. When you think of the things you are going to do in a day, if you hear yourself saying "I have to do...." or "I must do...." or "I should...." then you are living parts of your life according to what you think other people want you to do. Listen to your heart and ask yourself what you would really **love to be, to do and to have** in your life. Take some time to sit down and reflect on what really inspires you, what you want to achieve in this life and what difference you would like to make or service you would like to provide for others. It's impossible to put a wrong answer — they are yours and only you truly know what you want to dedicate your life to. Don't say "I don't know." — You are the only one who definitely does know. So, if you have never done this before, just start...make this your first draft — you have the power to change it whenever you like!

Once you get clear on what you really want in your life, these Life Priorities become your compass you can check in with every time an opportunity comes your way or there is a decision to make.

Reviewing your Life Priorities regularly (annually at the very least) helps ensure you are conscious of what you are doing with your life — after all you only get one go to live your life in your current body, so why not make sure you do as much of what you love as possible. We all leave a legacy when we leave the planet — why not leave a legacy you create on purpose rather than by accident?

Make sure you take the time to put something down for every area of your life. If there is an area you choose to ignore, you can be sure someone else will start running your life in that area. In fact other people can only overpower you if you choose to stay under educated and don't take action in an area. It is wise to ensure you pay enough attention to all areas of your life in which you would like to have fulfilment.

Now, go to a quiet place where you won't get interrupted, get comfortable, get focussed and write out your top Life Priorities in each of the areas of life.

# Inspired Life Scope

Use conscious intention and write a description of your inspired life...

SPIRITUAL

...........................................................................
...........................................................................
...........................................................................
...........................................................................
...........................................................................
...........................................................................
...........................................................................
...........................................................................

MENTAL / EDUCATION

...........................................................................
...........................................................................
...........................................................................
...........................................................................
...........................................................................
...........................................................................
...........................................................................
...........................................................................

VOCATIONAL / CAREER

...........................................................................
...........................................................................
...........................................................................
...........................................................................
...........................................................................
...........................................................................
...........................................................................

## FINANCIAL / SAVING & INVESTING

........................................................................................
........................................................................................
........................................................................................
........................................................................................
........................................................................................
........................................................................................
........................................................................................

## FAMILIAL / RELATIONSHIP

........................................................................................
........................................................................................
........................................................................................
........................................................................................
........................................................................................
........................................................................................
........................................................................................
........................................................................................

## SOCIAL / FRIENDS

........................................................................................
........................................................................................
........................................................................................
........................................................................................
........................................................................................
........................................................................................
........................................................................................
........................................................................................

## HEALTH & PHYSICAL APPEARANCE

........................................................................................
........................................................................................
........................................................................................
........................................................................................
........................................................................................
........................................................................................
........................................................................................
........................................................................................

# Inspired Life Masterpiece

Compose a visual masterpiece for your Inspired Life. Collages of images help your sub-conscious mind focus on what you want to create in your life. We remember everything as images, even words...how many times have you had to write a tricky word down so you could see what it looks like before you knew you had the spelling accurate? By creating a collage of images you give your subconscious mind high quality data and clarity about what you want to focus on achieving in your life.

Your subconscious mind is incredibly powerful and is running your mind and body more than 95% of the time so it is really, really, **really** important to let it know what you want to achieve in as much detail as you can!

The first step is to collect or draw images to use. If you can't find a picture of what you want in magazines, search the internet and print them out. Flick though images and notice when you see things that create a positive response in your heart — the stronger you feel inspired by the image, the more likely it is that it will be part of your future. The inspiration may be that you want to do the same as is in the image, or it may be that the image provokes in you the desire to make a positive difference in some way.

Drawing the images is also really powerful as your physical body is even more engaged in the creative process. Don't get hung up on the quality of your drawings or who might see them; you only need to represent the images you see in your mind with as much detail as you need to bring the full image back to mind. Play with colour in your drawings and for decorating your masterpiece. The more vividly you create your Inspired Life Masterpiece, the more easily you will hold it in mind.

Most importantly — have fun creating!

You are the only person who knows what you want — this is all about consciously creating an inspirational life for yourself. Look for the images of what you are prepared to work hard to bring into your life. Things that you are prepared to work through challenges to achieve — as humans we are wired with a desire to "play a bigger game" and we do that through overcoming challenges.

As in everything in life, you get back what you put in. If you only collect a whole lot of images of "stuff" that society projects as "the good life" and glue them in, you may fail to bring them into your life. It is fine to have nice "things" just ensure you also include images about your life purpose. To have your Inspired Life Masterpiece work, it is really important that you tune in at both a conscious and spiritual level to ensure you are including things that truly inspire you.

The soul will never be fulfilled through acquiring physical things.

When you include images that appeal to your authentic self you unleash the power of your imagination. Focus and quieten yourself then reflect on each image. Ask yourself what achieving or obtaining each thing will really mean to you. If it is important and you get a tear of inspiration, add it. If it feels superficial and just about "keeping up with the Jones'" let it go. Once you filter the images and connect with how they will help you fulfil your life purpose, your unconscious mind will automatically start asking incredibly creative and powerful questions that will help you move towards what you have included. Combinations of what you have included will start to stick in your mind and steer you towards making the vision real.

Ensure your Inspired Life Masterpiece includes images of things that are worth devoting your life to - because every day you get up and live, **you are always investing your life** in what you spend your time doing!

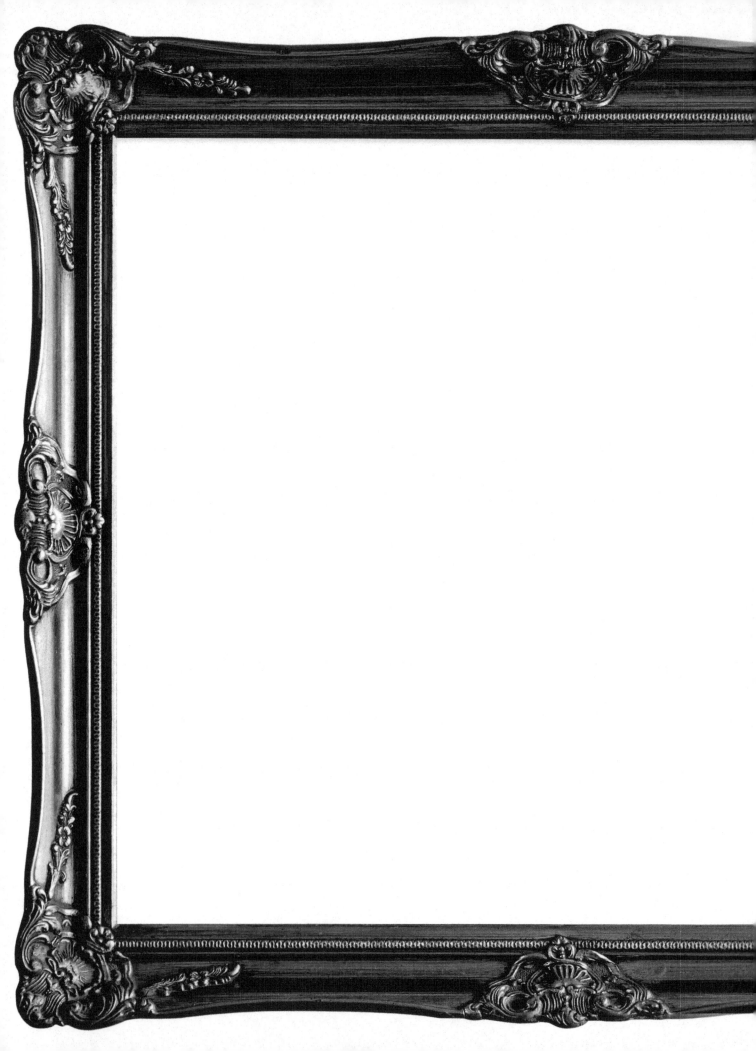

Vision
Board
<u>plan +
pleasure
to achieve
it.</u>

# Daily Journal Instructions

The individual day pages of this journal are set out
to assist you to focus on three key areas each day:
gratitude, your biggest daily challenge and your
highest intentions for the following day.

# Gratitude

The power of gratitude should never be underestimated. Taking some time to reflect and be grateful for your life creates amazing shifts in perception that help you lead a highly empowered life. Some people wish they were given all they want in life. In reality however, if we were only ever supported and given all that we ask for; life would soon become very boring and we would have no reason to grow or achieve.

When we start to look for, and really appreciate the benefits we receive from the challenges we face in our lives, we truly start to expand our perception of what is possible to achieve in our life. Our greatest growth occurs when there is a little chaos from challenge balanced by just enough support to keep us stable.

At the end of each day, take a few minutes to reflect on what you are truly grateful for in your life and how people have supported you to achieve your Life Priorities. Seeing the things you judge as positive is easy. Simply make a list so you can appreciate all of the ways you are supported. Reflect on your list and take a few moments to feel the appreciation in your body — when you are truly grateful, you will create a tear of inspiration in your eye.

If you are ever feeling low and having a self pity party, write a list of what you can be grateful for and keep going until you feel your energy shift back to the point where you can again appreciate what an amazing opportunity you have to experience and learn through being in a physical form. Start with the small things and work up from there. You will find them once you search. Also write down how the things you are grateful for will help you achieve your Life Priorities.

# Challenge

Next look for what your biggest challenge was in the day and find all of the ways that challenge will also assist you to achieve your Life Priorities. At first you may think there is no possible way a particular challenge helped you; look again and again. Think about how the challenge: taught you something; gave you a chance to practice a new skill; improved your character and/or strengthened your determination. Consider how the lesson learned or skill practised will help you in each of the areas of your life as you move forward. What will it help you achieve? What will it help you avoid that might cost you dearly in the future? For example if someone shouted at you and you felt hurt, it might mean you have practised resiliance

and that you decide to spend less time with that person. The next step is to ask yourself how spending less time with that person will be a benefit to you in all areas of your life. If you are not spending time with them, who would you prefer to spend that time with and how will that help you get what you want in life.

Find the benefits you received from each challenge and you will be able to shift your gratitude to a level of true inspiration and appreciation for the amazing universe in which we live.

# The Value of Intention

The final section to complete each evening is to take a few moments to write out your intentions for the following day. In the evening is the best time to set your priorities for the next day as it allows your subconscious mind to process it for you throughout the night and gain additional clarity before you take action the following day. Remember if you don't set your priorities for your day, someone else will.

Time is your most precious resource — once you have used it, you can never get it back! The more consciously you set your intention for activities you do, the easier it will be for you to achieve your Life Priorities. When you set your intentions daily and take action in line with them, you gain a greater sense of achievement and fulfilment in your life. Once you make this a habit, you will discover that it is such a powerful thing to do that you will wonder why you didn't start doing it sooner!

# Annual Calendar

| January | February | March | April | May | June |
|---|---|---|---|---|---|
| 1 | 1 | 1 | 1 | 1 | 1 |
| 2 | 2 | 2 | 2 | 2 | 2 |
| 3 | 3 | 3 | 3 | 3 | 3 |
| 4 | 4 | 4 | 4 | 4 | 4 |
| 5 | 5 | 5 | 5 | 5 | 5 |
| 6 | 6 | 6 | 6 | 6 | 6 |
| 7 | 7 | 7 | 7 | 7 | 7 |
| 8 | 8 | 8 | 8 | 8 | 8 |
| 9 | 9 | 9 | 9 | 9 | 9 |
| 10 | 10 | 10 | 10 | 10 | 10 |
| 11 | 11 | 11 | 11 | 11 | 11 |
| 12 | 12 | 12 | 12 | 12 | 12 |
| 13 | 13 | 13 | 13 | 13 | 13 |
| 14 | 14 | 14 | 14 | 14 | 14 |
| 15 | 15 | 15 | 15 | 15 | 15 |
| 16 | 16 | 16 | 16 | 16 | 16 |
| 17 | 17 | 17 | 17 | 17 | 17 |
| 18 | 18 | 18 | 18 | 18 | 18 |
| 19 | 19 | 19 | 19 | 19 | 19 |
| 20 | 20 | 20 | 20 | 20 | 20 |
| 21 | 21 | 21 | 21 | 21 | 21 |
| 22 | 22 | 22 | 22 | 22 | 22 |
| 23 | 23 | 23 | 23 | 23 | 23 |
| 24 | 24 | 24 | 24 | 24 | 24 |
| 25 | 25 | 25 | 25 | 25 | 25 |
| 26 | 26 | 26 | 26 | 26 | 26 |
| 27 | 27 | 27 | 27 | 27 | 27 |
| 28 | 28 | 28 | 28 | 28 | 28 |
| 29 | 29 | 29 | 29 | 29 | 29 |
| 30 | | 30 | 30 | 30 | 30 |
| 31 | | 31 | | 31 | |

| July | August | September | October | November | December |
|------|--------|-----------|---------|----------|----------|
| 1 | 1 | 1 | 1 | 1 | 1 |
| 2 | 2 | 2 | 2 | 2 | 2 |
| 3 | 3 | 3 | 3 | 3 | 3 |
| 4 | 4 | 4 | 4 | 4 | 4 |
| 5 | 5 | 5 | 5 | 5 | 5 |
| 6 | 6 | 6 | 6 | 6 | 6 |
| 7 | 7 | 7 | 7 | 7 | 7 |
| 8 | 8 | 8 | 8 | 8 | 8 |
| 9 | 9 | 9 | 9 | 9 | 9 |
| 10 | 10 | 10 | 10 | 10 | 10 |
| 11 | 11 | 11 | 11 | 11 | 11 |
| 12 | 12 | 12 | 12 | 12 | 12 |
| 13 | 13 | 13 | 13 | 13 | 13 |
| 14 | 14 | 14 | 14 | 14 | 14 |
| 15 | 15 | 15 | 15 | 15 | 15 |
| 16 | 16 | 16 | 16 | 16 | 16 |
| 17 | 17 | 17 | 17 | 17 | 17 |
| 18 | 18 | 18 | 18 | 18 | 18 |
| 19 | 19 | 19 | 19 | 19 | 19 |
| 20 | 20 | 20 | 20 | 20 | 20 |
| 21 | 21 | 21 | 21 | 21 | 21 |
| 22 | 22 | 22 | 22 | 22 | 22 |
| 23 | 23 | 23 | 23 | 23 | 23 |
| 24 | 24 | 24 | 24 | 24 | 24 |
| 25 | 25 | 25 | 25 | 25 | 25 |
| 26 | 26 | 26 | 26 | 26 | 26 |
| 27 | 27 | 27 | 27 | 27 | 27 |
| 28 | 28 | 28 | 28 | 28 | 28 |
| 29 | 29 | 29 | 29 | 29 | 29 |
| 30 | 30 | 30 | 30 | 30 | 30 |
| 31 | 31 | | 31 | | 31 |

# 12 Month Intention Plan

Another way to set powerful intentions for your life is to write a word story of this day one year from now as you intend to create it. Be specific and add details about every area of your life. Read it aloud to yourself and if possible to another person and notice how it feels when you reflect on what you have achieved in your life.

It is now ............................................. and I am so grateful that ..............................................................
(same date and month as the day you write this)

..................................................................................................................................................
..................................................................................................................................................
..................................................................................................................................................
..................................................................................................................................................
..................................................................................................................................................
..................................................................................................................................................
..................................................................................................................................................
..................................................................................................................................................
..................................................................................................................................................
..................................................................................................................................................
..................................................................................................................................................
..................................................................................................................................................
..................................................................................................................................................
..................................................................................................................................................
..................................................................................................................................................
..................................................................................................................................................
..................................................................................................................................................
..................................................................................................................................................
..................................................................................................................................................
..................................................................................................................................................
..................................................................................................................................................
..................................................................................................................................................
..................................................................................................................................................
..................................................................................................................................................
..................................................................................................................................................

## Monthly Intention Plan

Write the top priorities you intend to focus on in each area of your life during this month.

SPIRITUAL

..................................................................................................................
..................................................................................................................
..................................................................................................................
..................................................................................................................
..................................................................................................................
..................................................................................................................
..................................................................................................................

MENTAL / EDUCATION

..................................................................................................................
..................................................................................................................
..................................................................................................................
..................................................................................................................
..................................................................................................................
..................................................................................................................
..................................................................................................................

VOCATIONAL / CAREER

..................................................................................................................
..................................................................................................................
..................................................................................................................
..................................................................................................................
..................................................................................................................
..................................................................................................................
..................................................................................................................

## FINANCIAL / SAVING & INVESTING

..................................................................................................................................
..................................................................................................................................
..................................................................................................................................
..................................................................................................................................
..................................................................................................................................
..................................................................................................................................
..................................................................................................................................

## FAMILIAL / RELATIONSHIP

..................................................................................................................................
..................................................................................................................................
..................................................................................................................................
..................................................................................................................................
..................................................................................................................................
..................................................................................................................................
..................................................................................................................................
..................................................................................................................................

## SOCIAL / FRIENDS

..................................................................................................................................
..................................................................................................................................
..................................................................................................................................
..................................................................................................................................
..................................................................................................................................
..................................................................................................................................
..................................................................................................................................
..................................................................................................................................

## HEALTH & PHYSICAL APPEARANCE

..................................................................................................................................
..................................................................................................................................
..................................................................................................................................
..................................................................................................................................
..................................................................................................................................
..................................................................................................................................
..................................................................................................................................
..................................................................................................................................

*You think me a child of circumstances. I make my circumstances.*
— Ralph Waldo Emerson

## Daily Gratitude and Intention

Today I am grateful for:

....................................................................
....................................................................
....................................................................
....................................................................
....................................................................
....................................................................
....................................................................
....................................................................
....................................................................
....................................................................
....................................................................
....................................................................
....................................................................
....................................................................

Today's challenge and how it serves me to achieve my Life Priorities.

....................................................................
....................................................................
....................................................................
....................................................................
....................................................................

My highest Intentions for Tomorrow:

....................................................................
....................................................................
....................................................................
....................................................................
....................................................................

## Daily Gratitude and Intention

Today I am grateful for:

.............................................................................................

.............................................................................................

.............................................................................................

.............................................................................................

.............................................................................................

.............................................................................................

.............................................................................................

.............................................................................................

.............................................................................................

.............................................................................................

.............................................................................................

.............................................................................................

**Today's challenge** and how it serves me to achieve my Life Priorities.

.............................................................................................

.............................................................................................

.............................................................................................

.............................................................................................

.............................................................................................

My **highest Intentions** for Tomorrow:

.............................................................................................

.............................................................................................

.............................................................................................

.............................................................................................

.............................................................................................

# JAN 3

*A grateful mind is a great mind which eventually attracts to itself great things. — Plato*

## Daily Gratitude and Intention

Today I am grateful for:

........................................................................................................................

........................................................................................................................

........................................................................................................................

........................................................................................................................

........................................................................................................................

........................................................................................................................

........................................................................................................................

........................................................................................................................

........................................................................................................................

........................................................................................................................

........................................................................................................................

........................................................................................................................

Today's challenge and how it serves me to achieve my Life Priorities.

........................................................................................................................

........................................................................................................................

........................................................................................................................

........................................................................................................................

........................................................................................................................

My highest Intentions for Tomorrow:

........................................................................................................................

........................................................................................................................

........................................................................................................................

........................................................................................................................

........................................................................................................................

## Daily Gratitude and Intention

Today I am grateful for:

.........................................................................................................................
.........................................................................................................................
.........................................................................................................................
.........................................................................................................................
.........................................................................................................................
.........................................................................................................................
.........................................................................................................................
.........................................................................................................................
.........................................................................................................................
.........................................................................................................................
.........................................................................................................................
.........................................................................................................................
.........................................................................................................................
.........................................................................................................................

Today's challenge and how it serves me to achieve my Life Priorities.

.........................................................................................................................
.........................................................................................................................
.........................................................................................................................
.........................................................................................................................
.........................................................................................................................
.........................................................................................................................

My highest Intentions for Tomorrow:

.........................................................................................................................
.........................................................................................................................
.........................................................................................................................
.........................................................................................................................
.........................................................................................................................
.........................................................................................................................

# JAN 5

*A grateful person trusts enough to give life another chance, to stay open for surprises. — Brother David Steindal-Rast*

## Daily Gratitude and Intention

Today I am grateful for:

.......................................................................................................
.......................................................................................................
.......................................................................................................
.......................................................................................................
.......................................................................................................
.......................................................................................................
.......................................................................................................
.......................................................................................................
.......................................................................................................
.......................................................................................................
.......................................................................................................
.......................................................................................................
.......................................................................................................

Today's challenge and how it serves me to achieve my Life Priorities.

.......................................................................................................
.......................................................................................................
.......................................................................................................
.......................................................................................................
.......................................................................................................

My highest Intentions for Tomorrow:

.......................................................................................................
.......................................................................................................
.......................................................................................................
.......................................................................................................
.......................................................................................................

*A man's indebtedness is not virtue; his repayment is. Virtue begins when he dedicates himself actively to the job of gratitude.* — Ruth Benedict

# JAN 6

## Daily Gratitude and Intention

Today I am grateful for:

.........................................................................................
.........................................................................................
.........................................................................................
.........................................................................................
.........................................................................................
.........................................................................................
.........................................................................................
.........................................................................................
.........................................................................................
.........................................................................................
.........................................................................................
.........................................................................................
.........................................................................................
.........................................................................................

Today's challenge and how it serves me to achieve my Life Priorities.

.........................................................................................
.........................................................................................
.........................................................................................
.........................................................................................
.........................................................................................

My highest Intentions for Tomorrow:

.........................................................................................
.........................................................................................
.........................................................................................
.........................................................................................
.........................................................................................

# JAN 7

*A person however learned and qualified in his life's work in whom gratitude is absent, is devoid of that beauty of character which makes personality fragrant. — Hazrat Inayat Khan*

## Daily Gratitude and Intention

Today I am grateful for:

Today's challenge and how it serves me to achieve my Life Priorities.

My highest Intentions for Tomorrow:

*A simple grateful thought toward Heaven is the most complete prayer. — Gotthold Lessing*

# Daily Gratitude and Intention

Today I am grateful for:

.......................................................................................................................................
.......................................................................................................................................
.......................................................................................................................................
.......................................................................................................................................
.......................................................................................................................................
.......................................................................................................................................
.......................................................................................................................................
.......................................................................................................................................
.......................................................................................................................................
.......................................................................................................................................
.......................................................................................................................................
.......................................................................................................................................
.......................................................................................................................................
.......................................................................................................................................

Today's challenge and how it serves me to achieve my Life Priorities.

.......................................................................................................................................
.......................................................................................................................................
.......................................................................................................................................
.......................................................................................................................................
.......................................................................................................................................

My highest Intentions for Tomorrow:

.......................................................................................................................................
.......................................................................................................................................
.......................................................................................................................................
.......................................................................................................................................
.......................................................................................................................................

# JAN 9

*A thankful heart is not only the greatest virtue, but the parent of all the other virtues. — Cicero*

## Daily Gratitude and Intention

Today I am grateful for:

.......................................................................................................................................
.......................................................................................................................................
.......................................................................................................................................
.......................................................................................................................................
.......................................................................................................................................
.......................................................................................................................................
.......................................................................................................................................
.......................................................................................................................................
.......................................................................................................................................
.......................................................................................................................................
.......................................................................................................................................
.......................................................................................................................................
.......................................................................................................................................

Today's challenge and how it serves me to achieve my Life Priorities.

.......................................................................................................................................
.......................................................................................................................................
.......................................................................................................................................
.......................................................................................................................................
.......................................................................................................................................

My highest Intentions for Tomorrow:

.......................................................................................................................................
.......................................................................................................................................
.......................................................................................................................................
.......................................................................................................................................
.......................................................................................................................................

*Acknowledging the good that you already have in your life is the foundation for all abundance.* — *Eckhart Tolle*

## Daily Gratitude and Intention

Today I am grateful for:

..........................................................................................................................
..........................................................................................................................
..........................................................................................................................
..........................................................................................................................
..........................................................................................................................
..........................................................................................................................
..........................................................................................................................
..........................................................................................................................
..........................................................................................................................
..........................................................................................................................
..........................................................................................................................
..........................................................................................................................
..........................................................................................................................
..........................................................................................................................
..........................................................................................................................

Today's challenge and how it serves me to achieve my Life Priorities.

..........................................................................................................................
..........................................................................................................................
..........................................................................................................................
..........................................................................................................................
..........................................................................................................................
..........................................................................................................................

My highest Intentions for Tomorrow:

..........................................................................................................................
..........................................................................................................................
..........................................................................................................................
..........................................................................................................................
..........................................................................................................................

# JAN 11

## Daily Gratitude and Intention

Today I am grateful for:

.......................................................................................................
.......................................................................................................
.......................................................................................................
.......................................................................................................
.......................................................................................................
.......................................................................................................
.......................................................................................................
.......................................................................................................
.......................................................................................................
.......................................................................................................
.......................................................................................................
.......................................................................................................
.......................................................................................................

Today's challenge and how it serves me to achieve my Life Priorities.

.......................................................................................................
.......................................................................................................
.......................................................................................................
.......................................................................................................
.......................................................................................................

My highest Intentions for Tomorrow:

.......................................................................................................
.......................................................................................................
.......................................................................................................
.......................................................................................................
.......................................................................................................

*All sanity depends on this: that it should be a delight to feel the roughness of a carpet under smooth soles, a delight to feel heat strike the skin, a delight to stand upright, knowing the bones are moving easily under the flesh.*
*— Doris Lessing, The Golden Notebook*

# JAN 12

## Daily Gratitude and Intention

Today I am grateful for:

.......................................................................................................
.......................................................................................................
.......................................................................................................
.......................................................................................................
.......................................................................................................
.......................................................................................................
.......................................................................................................
.......................................................................................................
.......................................................................................................
.......................................................................................................
.......................................................................................................
.......................................................................................................
.......................................................................................................
.......................................................................................................

Today's challenge and how it serves me to achieve my Life Priorities.

.......................................................................................................
.......................................................................................................
.......................................................................................................
.......................................................................................................
.......................................................................................................
.......................................................................................................

My highest Intentions for Tomorrow:

.......................................................................................................
.......................................................................................................
.......................................................................................................
.......................................................................................................
.......................................................................................................

# JAN 13

*All that we behold is full of blessings.*
*— William Wordsworth*

## Daily Gratitude and Intention

Today I am grateful for:

....................................................................................................................
....................................................................................................................
....................................................................................................................
....................................................................................................................
....................................................................................................................
....................................................................................................................
....................................................................................................................
....................................................................................................................
....................................................................................................................
....................................................................................................................
....................................................................................................................
....................................................................................................................
....................................................................................................................

Today's challenge and how it serves me to achieve my Life Priorities.

....................................................................................................................
....................................................................................................................
....................................................................................................................
....................................................................................................................
....................................................................................................................

My highest Intentions for Tomorrow:

....................................................................................................................
....................................................................................................................
....................................................................................................................
....................................................................................................................
....................................................................................................................

*Although time seems to fly, it never travels faster than one day at a time. Each day is a new opportunity to live your life to the fullest. In each waking day, you will find scores of blessings and opportunities for positive change. Do not let your TODAY be stolen by the unchangeable past or the indefinite future! Today is a new day! — Steve Maraboli*

# JAN 14

## Daily Gratitude and Intention

Today I am grateful for:

..........................................................................................
..........................................................................................
..........................................................................................
..........................................................................................
..........................................................................................
..........................................................................................
..........................................................................................
..........................................................................................
..........................................................................................
..........................................................................................
..........................................................................................
..........................................................................................

Today's challenge and how it serves me to achieve my Life Priorities.

..........................................................................................
..........................................................................................
..........................................................................................
..........................................................................................

My highest Intentions for Tomorrow:

..........................................................................................
..........................................................................................
..........................................................................................
..........................................................................................

# JAN 15

## Daily Gratitude and Intention

Today I am grateful for:

...........................................................................................................................................................

...........................................................................................................................................................

...........................................................................................................................................................

...........................................................................................................................................................

...........................................................................................................................................................

...........................................................................................................................................................

...........................................................................................................................................................

...........................................................................................................................................................

...........................................................................................................................................................

...........................................................................................................................................................

...........................................................................................................................................................

...........................................................................................................................................................

...........................................................................................................................................................

Today's challenge and how it serves me to achieve my Life Priorities.

...........................................................................................................................................................

...........................................................................................................................................................

...........................................................................................................................................................

...........................................................................................................................................................

...........................................................................................................................................................

My highest Intentions for Tomorrow:

...........................................................................................................................................................

...........................................................................................................................................................

...........................................................................................................................................................

...........................................................................................................................................................

...........................................................................................................................................................

## Daily Gratitude and Intention

Today I am grateful for:

......................................................................................................................

......................................................................................................................

......................................................................................................................

......................................................................................................................

......................................................................................................................

......................................................................................................................

......................................................................................................................

......................................................................................................................

......................................................................................................................

......................................................................................................................

......................................................................................................................

......................................................................................................................

......................................................................................................................

......................................................................................................................

Today's challenge and how it serves me to achieve my Life Priorities.

......................................................................................................................

......................................................................................................................

......................................................................................................................

......................................................................................................................

......................................................................................................................

My highest Intentions for Tomorrow:

......................................................................................................................

......................................................................................................................

......................................................................................................................

......................................................................................................................

# JAN 17

*Appreciation can make a day, even change a life. Your willingness to put it into words is all that is necessary.*
*— Margaret Cousins*

## Daily Gratitude and Intention

Today I am grateful for:

.......................................................................
.......................................................................
.......................................................................
.......................................................................
.......................................................................
.......................................................................
.......................................................................
.......................................................................
.......................................................................
.......................................................................
.......................................................................
.......................................................................
.......................................................................
.......................................................................
.......................................................................

Today's challenge and how it serves me to achieve my Life Priorities.

.......................................................................
.......................................................................
.......................................................................
.......................................................................
.......................................................................

My highest Intentions for Tomorrow:

.......................................................................
.......................................................................
.......................................................................
.......................................................................
.......................................................................

## Daily Gratitude and Intention

Today I am grateful for:

........................................................................................................................

........................................................................................................................

........................................................................................................................

........................................................................................................................

........................................................................................................................

........................................................................................................................

........................................................................................................................

........................................................................................................................

........................................................................................................................

........................................................................................................................

........................................................................................................................

........................................................................................................................

........................................................................................................................

Today's challenge and how it serves me to achieve my Life Priorities.

........................................................................................................................

........................................................................................................................

........................................................................................................................

........................................................................................................................

........................................................................................................................

My highest Intentions for Tomorrow:

........................................................................................................................

........................................................................................................................

........................................................................................................................

........................................................................................................................

# JAN 19

## Daily Gratitude and Intention

Today I am grateful for:

.......................................................................................................
.......................................................................................................
.......................................................................................................
.......................................................................................................
.......................................................................................................
.......................................................................................................
.......................................................................................................
.......................................................................................................
.......................................................................................................
.......................................................................................................
.......................................................................................................
.......................................................................................................
.......................................................................................................
.......................................................................................................

**Today's challenge** and how it serves me to achieve my Life Priorities.

.......................................................................................................
.......................................................................................................
.......................................................................................................
.......................................................................................................
.......................................................................................................
.......................................................................................................

My **highest Intentions** for Tomorrow:

.......................................................................................................
.......................................................................................................
.......................................................................................................
.......................................................................................................
.......................................................................................................

## Daily Gratitude and Intention

Today I am grateful for:

........................................................................................

........................................................................................

........................................................................................

........................................................................................

........................................................................................

........................................................................................

........................................................................................

........................................................................................

........................................................................................

........................................................................................

........................................................................................

........................................................................................

........................................................................................

Today's challenge and how it serves me to achieve my Life Priorities.

........................................................................................

........................................................................................

........................................................................................

........................................................................................

........................................................................................

........................................................................................

My highest Intentions for Tomorrow:

........................................................................................

........................................................................................

........................................................................................

........................................................................................

........................................................................................

# JAN 21

## Daily Gratitude and Intention

Today I am grateful for:

..............................................................................................................
..............................................................................................................
..............................................................................................................
..............................................................................................................
..............................................................................................................
..............................................................................................................
..............................................................................................................
..............................................................................................................
..............................................................................................................
..............................................................................................................
..............................................................................................................
..............................................................................................................
..............................................................................................................
..............................................................................................................
..............................................................................................................
..............................................................................................................

Today's challenge and how it serves me to achieve my Life Priorities.

..............................................................................................................
..............................................................................................................
..............................................................................................................
..............................................................................................................
..............................................................................................................

My highest Intentions for Tomorrow:

..............................................................................................................
..............................................................................................................
..............................................................................................................
..............................................................................................................
..............................................................................................................

As each day comes to us refreshed and anew, so does my gratitude renews itself daily. The breaking of the sun over the horizon is my grateful heart dawning upon a blessed world.
— Terri Guillemets

# JAN 22

## Daily Gratitude and Intention

Today I am grateful for:

.......................................................................
.......................................................................
.......................................................................
.......................................................................
.......................................................................
.......................................................................
.......................................................................
.......................................................................
.......................................................................
.......................................................................
.......................................................................
.......................................................................
.......................................................................
.......................................................................

Today's challenge and how it serves me to achieve my Life Priorities.

.......................................................................
.......................................................................
.......................................................................
.......................................................................
.......................................................................

My highest Intentions for Tomorrow:

.......................................................................
.......................................................................
.......................................................................
.......................................................................
.......................................................................

# JAN 23

## Daily Gratitude and Intention

Today I am grateful for:

Today's challenge and how it serves me to achieve my Life Priorities.

My highest Intentions for Tomorrow:

## Daily Gratitude and Intention

Today I am grateful for:

........................................................................................................

........................................................................................................

........................................................................................................

........................................................................................................

........................................................................................................

........................................................................................................

........................................................................................................

........................................................................................................

........................................................................................................

........................................................................................................

........................................................................................................

........................................................................................................

........................................................................................................

Today's challenge and how it serves me to achieve my Life Priorities.

........................................................................................................

........................................................................................................

........................................................................................................

........................................................................................................

........................................................................................................

........................................................................................................

My highest Intentions for Tomorrow:

........................................................................................................

........................................................................................................

........................................................................................................

........................................................................................................

........................................................................................................

# JAN 25

## Daily Gratitude and Intention

Today I am grateful for:

..................................................................................................
..................................................................................................
..................................................................................................
..................................................................................................
..................................................................................................
..................................................................................................
..................................................................................................
..................................................................................................
..................................................................................................
..................................................................................................
..................................................................................................
..................................................................................................
..................................................................................................

Today's challenge and how it serves me to achieve my Life Priorities.

..................................................................................................
..................................................................................................
..................................................................................................
..................................................................................................
..................................................................................................

My highest Intentions for Tomorrow:

..................................................................................................
..................................................................................................
..................................................................................................
..................................................................................................
..................................................................................................

*Be anxious for nothing, but in everything by prayer and supplication, with thanksgiving, let your requests be made known to God. — The Bible Phil 4:6 NKJV*

# JAN 26

## Daily Gratitude and Intention

Today I am grateful for:

....................................................................
....................................................................
....................................................................
....................................................................
....................................................................
....................................................................
....................................................................
....................................................................
....................................................................
....................................................................
....................................................................
....................................................................
....................................................................
....................................................................

Today's challenge and how it serves me to achieve my Life Priorities.

....................................................................
....................................................................
....................................................................
....................................................................
....................................................................

My highest Intentions for Tomorrow:

....................................................................
....................................................................
....................................................................
....................................................................
....................................................................

# JAN 27

## Daily Gratitude and Intention

Today I am grateful for:

.............................................................................................................................................

.............................................................................................................................................

.............................................................................................................................................

.............................................................................................................................................

.............................................................................................................................................

.............................................................................................................................................

.............................................................................................................................................

.............................................................................................................................................

.............................................................................................................................................

.............................................................................................................................................

.............................................................................................................................................

.............................................................................................................................................

Today's challenge and how it serves me to achieve my Life Priorities.

.............................................................................................................................................

.............................................................................................................................................

.............................................................................................................................................

.............................................................................................................................................

.............................................................................................................................................

My highest Intentions for Tomorrow:

.............................................................................................................................................

.............................................................................................................................................

.............................................................................................................................................

.............................................................................................................................................

.............................................................................................................................................

## Daily Gratitude and Intention

Today I am grateful for:

.....................................................................................................................................
.....................................................................................................................................
.....................................................................................................................................
.....................................................................................................................................
.....................................................................................................................................
.....................................................................................................................................
.....................................................................................................................................
.....................................................................................................................................
.....................................................................................................................................
.....................................................................................................................................
.....................................................................................................................................
.....................................................................................................................................
.....................................................................................................................................
.....................................................................................................................................

Today's challenge and how it serves me to achieve my Life Priorities.

.....................................................................................................................................
.....................................................................................................................................
.....................................................................................................................................
.....................................................................................................................................
.....................................................................................................................................

My highest Intentions for Tomorrow:

.....................................................................................................................................
.....................................................................................................................................
.....................................................................................................................................
.....................................................................................................................................
.....................................................................................................................................

# JAN 29

## Daily Gratitude and Intention

Today I am grateful for:

......................................................................................................
......................................................................................................
......................................................................................................
......................................................................................................
......................................................................................................
......................................................................................................
......................................................................................................
......................................................................................................
......................................................................................................
......................................................................................................
......................................................................................................
......................................................................................................
......................................................................................................
......................................................................................................

Today's challenge and how it serves me to achieve my Life Priorities.

......................................................................................................
......................................................................................................
......................................................................................................
......................................................................................................
......................................................................................................

My highest Intentions for Tomorrow:

......................................................................................................
......................................................................................................
......................................................................................................
......................................................................................................
......................................................................................................

## Daily Gratitude and Intention

Today I am grateful for:

......................................................................................................

......................................................................................................

......................................................................................................

......................................................................................................

......................................................................................................

......................................................................................................

......................................................................................................

......................................................................................................

......................................................................................................

......................................................................................................

......................................................................................................

Today's challenge and how it serves me to achieve my Life Priorities.

......................................................................................................

......................................................................................................

......................................................................................................

......................................................................................................

......................................................................................................

My highest Intentions for Tomorrow:

......................................................................................................

......................................................................................................

......................................................................................................

......................................................................................................

# JAN 31

*Be happy, noble heart, be blessed for all the good
thou hast done and wilt do hereafter, and let my
gratitude remain in obscurity like your good deeds.
— Alexandre Dumas*

## Daily Gratitude and Intention

Today I am grateful for:

.............................................................................................
.............................................................................................
.............................................................................................
.............................................................................................
.............................................................................................
.............................................................................................
.............................................................................................
.............................................................................................
.............................................................................................
.............................................................................................

Today's challenge and how it serves me to achieve my Life Priorities.

.............................................................................................
.............................................................................................
.............................................................................................
.............................................................................................
.............................................................................................

My highest Intentions for Tomorrow:

.............................................................................................
.............................................................................................
.............................................................................................
.............................................................................................
.............................................................................................

The more you praise and celebrate
your life, the more there is in life
to celebrate

— Oprah Winfrey

# FEBRUARY

## Monthly Intention Plan

Write the top priorities you intend to focus on in each area of your life during this month.

SPIRITUAL

........................................................................................................
........................................................................................................
........................................................................................................
........................................................................................................
........................................................................................................
........................................................................................................
........................................................................................................
........................................................................................................

MENTAL / EDUCATION

........................................................................................................
........................................................................................................
........................................................................................................
........................................................................................................
........................................................................................................
........................................................................................................
........................................................................................................
........................................................................................................

VOCATIONAL / CAREER

........................................................................................................
........................................................................................................
........................................................................................................
........................................................................................................
........................................................................................................
........................................................................................................
........................................................................................................

## FINANCIAL / SAVING & INVESTING

............................................................................................................
............................................................................................................
............................................................................................................
............................................................................................................
............................................................................................................
............................................................................................................
............................................................................................................

## FAMILIAL / RELATIONSHIP

............................................................................................................
............................................................................................................
............................................................................................................
............................................................................................................
............................................................................................................
............................................................................................................
............................................................................................................
............................................................................................................

## SOCIAL / FRIENDS

............................................................................................................
............................................................................................................
............................................................................................................
............................................................................................................
............................................................................................................
............................................................................................................
............................................................................................................
............................................................................................................

## HEALTH & PHYSICAL APPEARANCE

............................................................................................................
............................................................................................................
............................................................................................................
............................................................................................................
............................................................................................................
............................................................................................................
............................................................................................................

# FEB 1

## Daily Gratitude and Intention

Today I am grateful for:

........................................................................
........................................................................
........................................................................
........................................................................
........................................................................
........................................................................
........................................................................
........................................................................
........................................................................
........................................................................
........................................................................
........................................................................
........................................................................
........................................................................
........................................................................
........................................................................
........................................................................

Today's challenge and how it serves me to achieve my Life Priorities.

........................................................................
........................................................................
........................................................................
........................................................................
........................................................................
........................................................................

My highest Intentions for Tomorrow:

........................................................................
........................................................................
........................................................................
........................................................................
........................................................................

*Because gratitude is the key to happiness, anything that undermines gratitude must undermine happiness.*
*— Dennis Prager*

# FEB 2

## Daily Gratitude and Intention

Today I am grateful for:

.................................................................................................

.................................................................................................

.................................................................................................

.................................................................................................

.................................................................................................

.................................................................................................

.................................................................................................

.................................................................................................

.................................................................................................

.................................................................................................

.................................................................................................

.................................................................................................

Today's challenge and how it serves me to achieve my Life Priorities.

.................................................................................................

.................................................................................................

.................................................................................................

.................................................................................................

.................................................................................................

My highest Intentions for Tomorrow:

.................................................................................................

.................................................................................................

.................................................................................................

.................................................................................................

*Being in the habit of saying "Thank you," of making sure that people receive attention so they know you value them, of not presuming that people will always be there—this is a good habit, regardless... make sure to give virtual and actual high-fives to those who rock and rock hard. — Sarah Wendell*

## Daily Gratitude and Intention

Today I am grateful for:

...............................................................................................................................

...............................................................................................................................

...............................................................................................................................

...............................................................................................................................

...............................................................................................................................

...............................................................................................................................

...............................................................................................................................

...............................................................................................................................

...............................................................................................................................

...............................................................................................................................

...............................................................................................................................

...............................................................................................................................

...............................................................................................................................

Today's challenge and how it serves me to achieve my Life Priorities.

...............................................................................................................................

...............................................................................................................................

...............................................................................................................................

...............................................................................................................................

...............................................................................................................................

My highest Intentions for Tomorrow:

...............................................................................................................................

...............................................................................................................................

...............................................................................................................................

...............................................................................................................................

*Best of all is it to preserve everything in a pure, still heart, and let there be for every pulse a thanksgiving, and for every breath a song. — Konrad von Gesner*

# Daily Gratitude and Intention

Today I am grateful for:

..................................................................................................................
..................................................................................................................
..................................................................................................................
..................................................................................................................
..................................................................................................................
..................................................................................................................
..................................................................................................................
..................................................................................................................
..................................................................................................................
..................................................................................................................
..................................................................................................................
..................................................................................................................
..................................................................................................................

Today's challenge and how it serves me to achieve my Life Priorities.

..................................................................................................................
..................................................................................................................
..................................................................................................................
..................................................................................................................
..................................................................................................................

My highest Intentions for Tomorrow:

..................................................................................................................
..................................................................................................................
..................................................................................................................
..................................................................................................................
..................................................................................................................

*Beth ceased to fear him from that moment, and sat there talking to him as cozily as if she had known him all her life, for love casts out fear, and gratitude can conquer pride.*
*— Louisa May Allcott*

## Daily Gratitude and Intention

Today I am grateful for:

........................................................................................
........................................................................................
........................................................................................
........................................................................................
........................................................................................
........................................................................................
........................................................................................
........................................................................................
........................................................................................
........................................................................................
........................................................................................
........................................................................................
........................................................................................

Today's challenge and how it serves me to achieve my Life Priorities.

........................................................................................
........................................................................................
........................................................................................
........................................................................................
........................................................................................
........................................................................................

My highest Intentions for Tomorrow:

........................................................................................
........................................................................................
........................................................................................
........................................................................................
........................................................................................

*Blessed is he who expects no gratitude, for he shall not be disappointed. — W.C. Bennett*

# Daily Gratitude and Intention

Today I am grateful for:

........................................................................................................
........................................................................................................
........................................................................................................
........................................................................................................
........................................................................................................
........................................................................................................
........................................................................................................
........................................................................................................
........................................................................................................
........................................................................................................
........................................................................................................
........................................................................................................
........................................................................................................

Today's challenge and how it serves me to achieve my Life Priorities.

........................................................................................................
........................................................................................................
........................................................................................................
........................................................................................................
........................................................................................................

My highest Intentions for Tomorrow:

........................................................................................................
........................................................................................................
........................................................................................................
........................................................................................................
........................................................................................................

# FEB 7

*But the value of gratitude does not consist solely in getting you more blessings in the future. Without gratitude you cannot long keep from dissatisfied thought regarding things as they are.*
*— Wallace Wattles*

## Daily Gratitude and Intention

Today I am grateful for:

.................................................................................................................
.................................................................................................................
.................................................................................................................
.................................................................................................................
.................................................................................................................
.................................................................................................................
.................................................................................................................
.................................................................................................................
.................................................................................................................
.................................................................................................................
.................................................................................................................
.................................................................................................................
.................................................................................................................

Today's challenge and how it serves me to achieve my Life Priorities.

.................................................................................................................
.................................................................................................................
.................................................................................................................
.................................................................................................................
.................................................................................................................

My highest Intentions for Tomorrow:

.................................................................................................................
.................................................................................................................
.................................................................................................................
.................................................................................................................

*Can you see the holiness in those things you take for granted—a paved road or a washing machine? If you concentrate on finding what is good in every situation, you will discover that your life will suddenly be filled with gratitude, a feeling that nurtures the soul.* — *Rabbi Harold Kushner*

# Daily Gratitude and Intention

Today I am grateful for:

.......................................................................................................................
.......................................................................................................................
.......................................................................................................................
.......................................................................................................................
.......................................................................................................................
.......................................................................................................................
.......................................................................................................................
.......................................................................................................................
.......................................................................................................................
.......................................................................................................................
.......................................................................................................................
.......................................................................................................................
.......................................................................................................................
.......................................................................................................................

Today's challenge and how it serves me to achieve my Life Priorities.

.......................................................................................................................
.......................................................................................................................
.......................................................................................................................
.......................................................................................................................
.......................................................................................................................

My highest Intentions for Tomorrow:

.......................................................................................................................
.......................................................................................................................
.......................................................................................................................
.......................................................................................................................
.......................................................................................................................

# FEB 9

## Daily Gratitude and Intention

Today I am grateful for:

.............................................................................................................
.............................................................................................................
.............................................................................................................
.............................................................................................................
.............................................................................................................
.............................................................................................................
.............................................................................................................
.............................................................................................................
.............................................................................................................
.............................................................................................................
.............................................................................................................
.............................................................................................................
.............................................................................................................
.............................................................................................................
.............................................................................................................

Today's challenge and how it serves me to achieve my Life Priorities.

.............................................................................................................
.............................................................................................................
.............................................................................................................
.............................................................................................................
.............................................................................................................

My highest Intentions for Tomorrow:

.............................................................................................................
.............................................................................................................
.............................................................................................................
.............................................................................................................
.............................................................................................................

*Christ himself wrote nothing, but furnished endless material for books and songs of gratitude and praise.*
*— Philip Schaff*

# FEB 10

## Daily Gratitude and Intention

Today I am grateful for:

..................................................................................................
..................................................................................................
..................................................................................................
..................................................................................................
..................................................................................................
..................................................................................................
..................................................................................................
..................................................................................................
..................................................................................................
..................................................................................................
..................................................................................................
..................................................................................................
..................................................................................................

Today's challenge and how it serves me to achieve my Life Priorities.

..................................................................................................
..................................................................................................
..................................................................................................
..................................................................................................
..................................................................................................

My highest Intentions for Tomorrow:

..................................................................................................
..................................................................................................
..................................................................................................
..................................................................................................
..................................................................................................

# FEB 11

## Daily Gratitude and Intention

Today I am grateful for:

.................................................................................................................
.................................................................................................................
.................................................................................................................
.................................................................................................................
.................................................................................................................
.................................................................................................................
.................................................................................................................
.................................................................................................................
.................................................................................................................
.................................................................................................................
.................................................................................................................
.................................................................................................................
.................................................................................................................

Today's challenge and how it serves me to achieve my Life Priorities.

.................................................................................................................
.................................................................................................................
.................................................................................................................
.................................................................................................................
.................................................................................................................

My highest Intentions for Tomorrow:

.................................................................................................................
.................................................................................................................
.................................................................................................................
.................................................................................................................
.................................................................................................................

*Cultivate the habit of being grateful for every good thing that comes to you, and to give thanks continuously. And because all things have contributed to your advancement, you should include all things in your gratitude.* — *Ralph Waldo Emerson*

# FEB 12

## Daily Gratitude and Intention

Today I am grateful for:

.......................................................................................................

.......................................................................................................

.......................................................................................................

.......................................................................................................

.......................................................................................................

.......................................................................................................

.......................................................................................................

.......................................................................................................

.......................................................................................................

.......................................................................................................

.......................................................................................................

.......................................................................................................

.......................................................................................................

.......................................................................................................

**Today's challenge** and how it serves me to achieve my Life Priorities.

.......................................................................................................

.......................................................................................................

.......................................................................................................

.......................................................................................................

.......................................................................................................

My **highest Intentions** for Tomorrow:

.......................................................................................................

.......................................................................................................

.......................................................................................................

.......................................................................................................

.......................................................................................................

# FEB 13

## Daily Gratitude and Intention

Today I am grateful for:

........................................................................................................

........................................................................................................

........................................................................................................

........................................................................................................

........................................................................................................

........................................................................................................

........................................................................................................

........................................................................................................

........................................................................................................

........................................................................................................

........................................................................................................

........................................................................................................

........................................................................................................

Today's challenge and how it serves me to achieve my Life Priorities.

........................................................................................................

........................................................................................................

........................................................................................................

........................................................................................................

........................................................................................................

........................................................................................................

My highest Intentions for Tomorrow:

........................................................................................................

........................................................................................................

........................................................................................................

........................................................................................................

........................................................................................................

*Divide the constant tide and random noisiness of energetic flow, with conscious recurring moments of empty mind, solitude, gratitude and deep... slow... breathing. Of this, the natural law of self-preservation demands. — T.F. Hodge*

# Daily Gratitude and Intention

Today I am grateful for:

.................................................................................................................
.................................................................................................................
.................................................................................................................
.................................................................................................................
.................................................................................................................
.................................................................................................................
.................................................................................................................
.................................................................................................................
.................................................................................................................
.................................................................................................................
.................................................................................................................
.................................................................................................................
.................................................................................................................

Today's challenge and how it serves me to achieve my Life Priorities.

.................................................................................................................
.................................................................................................................
.................................................................................................................
.................................................................................................................
.................................................................................................................

My highest Intentions for Tomorrow:

.................................................................................................................
.................................................................................................................
.................................................................................................................
.................................................................................................................
.................................................................................................................

# FEB 15

## Daily Gratitude and Intention

Today I am grateful for:

........................................................................................
........................................................................................
........................................................................................
........................................................................................
........................................................................................
........................................................................................
........................................................................................
........................................................................................
........................................................................................
........................................................................................
........................................................................................
........................................................................................

Today's challenge and how it serves me to achieve my Life Priorities.

........................................................................................
........................................................................................
........................................................................................
........................................................................................
........................................................................................

My highest Intentions for Tomorrow:

........................................................................................
........................................................................................
........................................................................................
........................................................................................
........................................................................................

*Do not take anything for granted — not one smile or one person or one rainbow or one breath, or one night in your cozy bed. — Terri Guillemets*

## Daily Gratitude and Intention

Today I am grateful for:

.......................................................................................................
.......................................................................................................
.......................................................................................................
.......................................................................................................
.......................................................................................................
.......................................................................................................
.......................................................................................................
.......................................................................................................
.......................................................................................................
.......................................................................................................
.......................................................................................................
.......................................................................................................
.......................................................................................................

Today's challenge and how it serves me to achieve my Life Priorities.

.......................................................................................................
.......................................................................................................
.......................................................................................................
.......................................................................................................
.......................................................................................................

My highest Intentions for Tomorrow:

.......................................................................................................
.......................................................................................................
.......................................................................................................
.......................................................................................................

# FEB 17

## Daily Gratitude and Intention

Today I am grateful for:

...........................................................................................................
...........................................................................................................
...........................................................................................................
...........................................................................................................
...........................................................................................................
...........................................................................................................
...........................................................................................................
...........................................................................................................
...........................................................................................................
...........................................................................................................
...........................................................................................................
...........................................................................................................
...........................................................................................................

Today's challenge and how it serves me to achieve my Life Priorities.

...........................................................................................................
...........................................................................................................
...........................................................................................................
...........................................................................................................
...........................................................................................................

My highest Intentions for Tomorrow:

...........................................................................................................
...........................................................................................................
...........................................................................................................
...........................................................................................................
...........................................................................................................

*Don't overlook the wonder of the ordinary.*
*— Anonymous*

## Daily Gratitude and Intention

Today I am grateful for:

.........................................................................................
.........................................................................................
.........................................................................................
.........................................................................................
.........................................................................................
.........................................................................................
.........................................................................................
.........................................................................................
.........................................................................................
.........................................................................................
.........................................................................................
.........................................................................................
.........................................................................................

Today's challenge and how it serves me to achieve my Life Priorities.

.........................................................................................
.........................................................................................
.........................................................................................
.........................................................................................
.........................................................................................

My highest Intentions for Tomorrow:

.........................................................................................
.........................................................................................
.........................................................................................
.........................................................................................
.........................................................................................

# FEB 19

*Don't pray when it rains if you don't pray when the sun shines.* — Satchell Paige

## Daily Gratitude and Intention

Today I am grateful for:

Today's challenge and how it serves me to achieve my Life Priorities.

My highest Intentions for Tomorrow:

*Enjoy the little things, for one day you may look back and realize they were the big things. — Robert Brault*

## Daily Gratitude and Intention

Today I am grateful for:

........................................................................................................
........................................................................................................
........................................................................................................
........................................................................................................
........................................................................................................
........................................................................................................
........................................................................................................
........................................................................................................
........................................................................................................
........................................................................................................
........................................................................................................
........................................................................................................
........................................................................................................

Today's challenge and how it serves me to achieve my Life Priorities.

........................................................................................................
........................................................................................................
........................................................................................................
........................................................................................................
........................................................................................................

My highest Intentions for Tomorrow:

........................................................................................................
........................................................................................................
........................................................................................................
........................................................................................................
........................................................................................................

# FEB 21

## Daily Gratitude and Intention

Today I am grateful for:

.................................................................................................
.................................................................................................
.................................................................................................
.................................................................................................
.................................................................................................
.................................................................................................
.................................................................................................
.................................................................................................
.................................................................................................
.................................................................................................
.................................................................................................
.................................................................................................

Today's challenge and how it serves me to achieve my Life Priorities.

.................................................................................................
.................................................................................................
.................................................................................................
.................................................................................................
.................................................................................................

My highest Intentions for Tomorrow:

.................................................................................................
.................................................................................................
.................................................................................................
.................................................................................................
.................................................................................................

## Daily Gratitude and Intention

Today I am grateful for:

.......................................................................................................................................
.......................................................................................................................................
.......................................................................................................................................
.......................................................................................................................................
.......................................................................................................................................
.......................................................................................................................................
.......................................................................................................................................
.......................................................................................................................................
.......................................................................................................................................
.......................................................................................................................................
.......................................................................................................................................
.......................................................................................................................................
.......................................................................................................................................
.......................................................................................................................................

Today's challenge and how it serves me to achieve my Life Priorities.

.......................................................................................................................................
.......................................................................................................................................
.......................................................................................................................................
.......................................................................................................................................
.......................................................................................................................................

My highest Intentions for Tomorrow:

.......................................................................................................................................
.......................................................................................................................................
.......................................................................................................................................
.......................................................................................................................................
.......................................................................................................................................

# FEB 23

## Daily Gratitude and Intention

Today I am grateful for:

........................................................................................
........................................................................................
........................................................................................
........................................................................................
........................................................................................
........................................................................................
........................................................................................
........................................................................................
........................................................................................
........................................................................................
........................................................................................
........................................................................................
........................................................................................
........................................................................................
........................................................................................

Today's challenge and how it serves me to achieve my Life Priorities.

........................................................................................
........................................................................................
........................................................................................
........................................................................................
........................................................................................

My highest Intentions for Tomorrow:

........................................................................................
........................................................................................
........................................................................................
........................................................................................
........................................................................................

*Every professional athlete owes a debt of gratitude to the fans and management, and pays an installment every time he plays. He should never miss a payment. — Bobby Hull*

# FEB 24

## Daily Gratitude and Intention

Today I am grateful for:

.......................................................................................
.......................................................................................
.......................................................................................
.......................................................................................
.......................................................................................
.......................................................................................
.......................................................................................
.......................................................................................
.......................................................................................
.......................................................................................
.......................................................................................
.......................................................................................
.......................................................................................

Today's challenge and how it serves me to achieve my Life Priorities.

.......................................................................................
.......................................................................................
.......................................................................................
.......................................................................................
.......................................................................................

My highest Intentions for Tomorrow:

.......................................................................................
.......................................................................................
.......................................................................................
.......................................................................................

# FEB 25

## Daily Gratitude and Intention

Today I am grateful for:

..............................................................................................
..............................................................................................
..............................................................................................
..............................................................................................
..............................................................................................
..............................................................................................
..............................................................................................
..............................................................................................
..............................................................................................
..............................................................................................
..............................................................................................
..............................................................................................
..............................................................................................

Today's challenge and how it serves me to achieve my Life Priorities.

..............................................................................................
..............................................................................................
..............................................................................................
..............................................................................................
..............................................................................................

My highest Intentions for Tomorrow:

..............................................................................................
..............................................................................................
..............................................................................................
..............................................................................................
..............................................................................................

*Everything we do should be a result of our gratitude for what God has done for us. — Lauryn Hill*

# Daily Gratitude and Intention

Today I am grateful for:

.................................................................................................................

.................................................................................................................

.................................................................................................................

.................................................................................................................

.................................................................................................................

.................................................................................................................

.................................................................................................................

.................................................................................................................

.................................................................................................................

.................................................................................................................

.................................................................................................................

.................................................................................................................

Today's challenge and how it serves me to achieve my Life Priorities.

.................................................................................................................

.................................................................................................................

.................................................................................................................

.................................................................................................................

.................................................................................................................

My highest Intentions for Tomorrow:

.................................................................................................................

.................................................................................................................

.................................................................................................................

.................................................................................................................

.................................................................................................................

# FEB 27

*Expressing gratitude is a natural state of being and reminds us that we are all connected.*
*— Valerie Elster*

## Daily Gratitude and Intention

Today I am grateful for:

..................................................................................................
..................................................................................................
..................................................................................................
..................................................................................................
..................................................................................................
..................................................................................................
..................................................................................................
..................................................................................................
..................................................................................................
..................................................................................................
..................................................................................................
..................................................................................................
..................................................................................................
..................................................................................................

Today's challenge and how it serves me to achieve my Life Priorities.

..................................................................................................
..................................................................................................
..................................................................................................
..................................................................................................
..................................................................................................

My highest Intentions for Tomorrow:

..................................................................................................
..................................................................................................
..................................................................................................
..................................................................................................
..................................................................................................

*Fearing to lose what you have is not the same as appreciation. You have to take a step beyond that.*
*— Terri Guillemets*

# FEB 28

## Daily Gratitude and Intention

Today I am grateful for:

.........................................................................................................................................

.........................................................................................................................................

.........................................................................................................................................

.........................................................................................................................................

.........................................................................................................................................

.........................................................................................................................................

.........................................................................................................................................

.........................................................................................................................................

.........................................................................................................................................

.........................................................................................................................................

.........................................................................................................................................

.........................................................................................................................................

Today's challenge and how it serves me to achieve my Life Priorities.

.........................................................................................................................................

.........................................................................................................................................

.........................................................................................................................................

.........................................................................................................................................

.........................................................................................................................................

My highest Intentions for Tomorrow:

.........................................................................................................................................

.........................................................................................................................................

.........................................................................................................................................

.........................................................................................................................................

# FEB 29

## Daily Gratitude and Intention

Today I am grateful for:

..............................................................................................................................
..............................................................................................................................
..............................................................................................................................
..............................................................................................................................
..............................................................................................................................
..............................................................................................................................
..............................................................................................................................
..............................................................................................................................
..............................................................................................................................
..............................................................................................................................
..............................................................................................................................
..............................................................................................................................
..............................................................................................................................

Today's challenge and how it serves me to achieve my Life Priorities.

..............................................................................................................................
..............................................................................................................................
..............................................................................................................................
..............................................................................................................................
..............................................................................................................................
..............................................................................................................................

My highest Intentions for Tomorrow:

..............................................................................................................................
..............................................................................................................................
..............................................................................................................................
..............................................................................................................................
..............................................................................................................................
..............................................................................................................................

He is a wise man who does not
grieve for the things which
he has not, but rejoices
for those which
he has.

— Epictetus

# MARCH

## Monthly Intention Plan

Write the top priorities you intend to focus on in each area of your life during this month.

SPIRITUAL

..................................................................................................................
..................................................................................................................
..................................................................................................................
..................................................................................................................
..................................................................................................................
..................................................................................................................
..................................................................................................................

MENTAL / EDUCATION

..................................................................................................................
..................................................................................................................
..................................................................................................................
..................................................................................................................
..................................................................................................................
..................................................................................................................
..................................................................................................................

VOCATIONAL / CAREER

..................................................................................................................
..................................................................................................................
..................................................................................................................
..................................................................................................................
..................................................................................................................
..................................................................................................................
..................................................................................................................

## FINANCIAL / SAVING & INVESTING

........................................................................................................................................
........................................................................................................................................
........................................................................................................................................
........................................................................................................................................
........................................................................................................................................
........................................................................................................................................

## FAMILIAL / RELATIONSHIP

........................................................................................................................................
........................................................................................................................................
........................................................................................................................................
........................................................................................................................................
........................................................................................................................................
........................................................................................................................................

## SOCIAL / FRIENDS

........................................................................................................................................
........................................................................................................................................
........................................................................................................................................
........................................................................................................................................
........................................................................................................................................
........................................................................................................................................

## HEALTH & PHYSICAL APPEARANCE

........................................................................................................................................
........................................................................................................................................
........................................................................................................................................
........................................................................................................................................
........................................................................................................................................
........................................................................................................................................

# MAR 1

## Daily Gratitude and Intention

Today I am grateful for:

.........................................................................................
.........................................................................................
.........................................................................................
.........................................................................................
.........................................................................................
.........................................................................................
.........................................................................................
.........................................................................................
.........................................................................................
.........................................................................................
.........................................................................................
.........................................................................................
.........................................................................................
.........................................................................................

Today's challenge and how it serves me to achieve my Life Priorities.

.........................................................................................
.........................................................................................
.........................................................................................
.........................................................................................
.........................................................................................

My highest Intentions for Tomorrow:

.........................................................................................
.........................................................................................
.........................................................................................
.........................................................................................
.........................................................................................

*Feeling gratitude and not expressing it is like wrapping a present and not giving it. — William Arthur Ward*

# Daily Gratitude and Intention

Today I am grateful for:

..................................................................................................................................
..................................................................................................................................
..................................................................................................................................
..................................................................................................................................
..................................................................................................................................
..................................................................................................................................
..................................................................................................................................
..................................................................................................................................
..................................................................................................................................
..................................................................................................................................
..................................................................................................................................
..................................................................................................................................

Today's challenge and how it serves me to achieve my Life Priorities.

..................................................................................................................................
..................................................................................................................................
..................................................................................................................................
..................................................................................................................................
..................................................................................................................................

My highest Intentions for Tomorrow:

..................................................................................................................................
..................................................................................................................................
..................................................................................................................................
..................................................................................................................................
..................................................................................................................................

# MAR 3

## Daily Gratitude and Intention

Today I am grateful for:

..........................................................................................
..........................................................................................
..........................................................................................
..........................................................................................
..........................................................................................
..........................................................................................
..........................................................................................
..........................................................................................
..........................................................................................
..........................................................................................
..........................................................................................
..........................................................................................
..........................................................................................

Today's challenge and how it serves me to achieve my Life Priorities.

..........................................................................................
..........................................................................................
..........................................................................................
..........................................................................................
..........................................................................................

My highest Intentions for Tomorrow:

..........................................................................................
..........................................................................................
..........................................................................................
..........................................................................................
..........................................................................................

*Find the light. Reach for it. Live for it. Pull yourself up by it. Gratitude always makes for straighter, taller trees.*
*— Al R. Young*

# MAR 4

## Daily Gratitude and Intention

Today I am grateful for:

........................................................................................
........................................................................................
........................................................................................
........................................................................................
........................................................................................
........................................................................................
........................................................................................
........................................................................................
........................................................................................
........................................................................................
........................................................................................
........................................................................................
........................................................................................

**Today's challenge** and how it serves me to achieve my Life Priorities.

........................................................................................
........................................................................................
........................................................................................
........................................................................................
........................................................................................
........................................................................................

My **highest Intentions** for Tomorrow:

........................................................................................
........................................................................................
........................................................................................
........................................................................................
........................................................................................

# MAR 5

*For each new morning with its light, For rest and shelter of the night, For health and food, for love and friends, For everything. Thy goodness sends. — Ralph Waldo Emerson*

## Daily Gratitude and Intention

Today I am grateful for:

..................................................................................................................................
..................................................................................................................................
..................................................................................................................................
..................................................................................................................................
..................................................................................................................................
..................................................................................................................................
..................................................................................................................................
..................................................................................................................................
..................................................................................................................................
..................................................................................................................................
..................................................................................................................................
..................................................................................................................................
..................................................................................................................................

Today's challenge and how it serves me to achieve my Life Priorities.

..................................................................................................................................
..................................................................................................................................
..................................................................................................................................
..................................................................................................................................
..................................................................................................................................

My highest Intentions for Tomorrow:

..................................................................................................................................
..................................................................................................................................
..................................................................................................................................
..................................................................................................................................
..................................................................................................................................

## Daily Gratitude and Intention

Today I am grateful for:

.....................................................................
.....................................................................
.....................................................................
.....................................................................
.....................................................................
.....................................................................
.....................................................................
.....................................................................
.....................................................................
.....................................................................
.....................................................................
.....................................................................
.....................................................................

Today's challenge and how it serves me to achieve my Life Priorities.

.....................................................................
.....................................................................
.....................................................................
.....................................................................
.....................................................................

My highest Intentions for Tomorrow:

.....................................................................
.....................................................................
.....................................................................
.....................................................................
.....................................................................

# MAR 7

## Daily Gratitude and Intention

Today I am grateful for:

..................................................................................................................................
..................................................................................................................................
..................................................................................................................................
..................................................................................................................................
..................................................................................................................................
..................................................................................................................................
..................................................................................................................................
..................................................................................................................................
..................................................................................................................................
..................................................................................................................................
..................................................................................................................................
..................................................................................................................................

Today's challenge and how it serves me to achieve my Life Priorities.

..................................................................................................................................
..................................................................................................................................
..................................................................................................................................
..................................................................................................................................
..................................................................................................................................

My highest Intentions for Tomorrow:

..................................................................................................................................
..................................................................................................................................
..................................................................................................................................
..................................................................................................................................
..................................................................................................................................

*Free yourself from the complexities and drama of your life. Simplify. Look within. Within ourselves we all have the gifts and talents we need to fulfill the purpose we've been blessed with. — Steve Maraboli*

# Daily Gratitude and Intention

Today I am grateful for:

.................................................................................................
.................................................................................................
.................................................................................................
.................................................................................................
.................................................................................................
.................................................................................................
.................................................................................................
.................................................................................................
.................................................................................................
.................................................................................................
.................................................................................................
.................................................................................................
.................................................................................................

Today's challenge and how it serves me to achieve my Life Priorities.

.................................................................................................
.................................................................................................
.................................................................................................
.................................................................................................
.................................................................................................

My highest Intentions for Tomorrow:

.................................................................................................
.................................................................................................
.................................................................................................
.................................................................................................
.................................................................................................

# MAR 9

## Daily Gratitude and Intention

Today I am grateful for:

........................................................................................
........................................................................................
........................................................................................
........................................................................................
........................................................................................
........................................................................................
........................................................................................
........................................................................................
........................................................................................
........................................................................................
........................................................................................
........................................................................................
........................................................................................

Today's challenge and how it serves me to achieve my Life Priorities.

........................................................................................
........................................................................................
........................................................................................
........................................................................................
........................................................................................
........................................................................................

My highest Intentions for Tomorrow:

........................................................................................
........................................................................................
........................................................................................
........................................................................................
........................................................................................

*Go to foreign countries and you will get to know the good things one possesses at home.*
*— Johann Wolfgang Von Goethe*

# MAR 10

## Daily Gratitude and Intention

Today I am grateful for:

..............................................................................................
..............................................................................................
..............................................................................................
..............................................................................................
..............................................................................................
..............................................................................................
..............................................................................................
..............................................................................................
..............................................................................................
..............................................................................................
..............................................................................................
..............................................................................................

Today's challenge and how it serves me to achieve my Life Priorities.

..............................................................................................
..............................................................................................
..............................................................................................
..............................................................................................
..............................................................................................

My highest Intentions for Tomorrow:

..............................................................................................
..............................................................................................
..............................................................................................
..............................................................................................
..............................................................................................

# MAR 11

## Daily Gratitude and Intention

Today I am grateful for:

........................................................................................................
........................................................................................................
........................................................................................................
........................................................................................................
........................................................................................................
........................................................................................................
........................................................................................................
........................................................................................................
........................................................................................................
........................................................................................................
........................................................................................................
........................................................................................................
........................................................................................................

Today's challenge and how it serves me to achieve my Life Priorities.

........................................................................................................
........................................................................................................
........................................................................................................
........................................................................................................
........................................................................................................

My highest Intentions for Tomorrow:

........................................................................................................
........................................................................................................
........................................................................................................
........................................................................................................
........................................................................................................

*Got no checkbooks, got no banks. Still I'd like to express my thanks—I've got the sun in the mornin' and the moon at night.* — Irving Berlin

# MAR 12

## Daily Gratitude and Intention

Today I am grateful for:

........................................................................................
........................................................................................
........................................................................................
........................................................................................
........................................................................................
........................................................................................
........................................................................................
........................................................................................
........................................................................................
........................................................................................
........................................................................................
........................................................................................
........................................................................................

**Today's challenge** and how it serves me to achieve my Life Priorities.

........................................................................................
........................................................................................
........................................................................................
........................................................................................
........................................................................................

My highest **Intentions** for Tomorrow:

........................................................................................
........................................................................................
........................................................................................
........................................................................................
........................................................................................

# MAR 13

## Daily Gratitude and Intention

Today I am grateful for:

........................................................................
........................................................................
........................................................................
........................................................................
........................................................................
........................................................................
........................................................................
........................................................................
........................................................................
........................................................................
........................................................................
........................................................................

Today's challenge and how it serves me to achieve my Life Priorities.

........................................................................
........................................................................
........................................................................
........................................................................
........................................................................

My highest Intentions for Tomorrow:

........................................................................
........................................................................
........................................................................
........................................................................
........................................................................

Gratefulness is the key to a happy life that we hold in our hands, because if we are not grateful, then no matter how much we have we will not be happy — because we will always want to have something else or something more. — David Steindl-Rast

## Daily Gratitude and Intention

Today I am grateful for:

.......................................................................................................................
.......................................................................................................................
.......................................................................................................................
.......................................................................................................................
.......................................................................................................................
.......................................................................................................................
.......................................................................................................................
.......................................................................................................................
.......................................................................................................................
.......................................................................................................................
.......................................................................................................................
.......................................................................................................................
.......................................................................................................................
.......................................................................................................................

Today's challenge and how it serves me to achieve my Life Priorities.

.......................................................................................................................
.......................................................................................................................
.......................................................................................................................
.......................................................................................................................
.......................................................................................................................

My highest Intentions for Tomorrow:

.......................................................................................................................
.......................................................................................................................
.......................................................................................................................
.......................................................................................................................
.......................................................................................................................

# MAR 15

## Daily Gratitude and Intention

Today I am grateful for:

..................................................................................
..................................................................................
..................................................................................
..................................................................................
..................................................................................
..................................................................................
..................................................................................
..................................................................................
..................................................................................
..................................................................................
..................................................................................
..................................................................................
..................................................................................
..................................................................................

Today's challenge and how it serves me to achieve my Life Priorities.

..................................................................................
..................................................................................
..................................................................................
..................................................................................
..................................................................................

My highest Intentions for Tomorrow:

..................................................................................
..................................................................................
..................................................................................
..................................................................................
..................................................................................

*Gratitude always comes into play; research shows that people are happier if they are grateful for the positive things in their lives, rather than worrying about what might be missing. — Dan Buettner*

# MAR 16

## Daily Gratitude and Intention

Today I am grateful for:

Today's challenge and how it serves me to achieve my Life Priorities.

My highest Intentions for Tomorrow:

# MAR 17

## Daily Gratitude and Intention

Today I am grateful for:

.....................................................................................................................................................

.....................................................................................................................................................

.....................................................................................................................................................

.....................................................................................................................................................

.....................................................................................................................................................

.....................................................................................................................................................

.....................................................................................................................................................

.....................................................................................................................................................

.....................................................................................................................................................

.....................................................................................................................................................

.....................................................................................................................................................

.....................................................................................................................................................

.....................................................................................................................................................

**Today's challenge** and how it serves me to achieve my Life Priorities.

.....................................................................................................................................................

.....................................................................................................................................................

.....................................................................................................................................................

.....................................................................................................................................................

.....................................................................................................................................................

.....................................................................................................................................................

My **highest Intentions** for Tomorrow:

.....................................................................................................................................................

.....................................................................................................................................................

.....................................................................................................................................................

.....................................................................................................................................................

.....................................................................................................................................................

*Gratitude becomes spiritual, a spiritual virtue and a spiritual emotion, when we are moved in our response by a God-centered view of the three: gift, recipient, and giver. — Ray A.*

## Daily Gratitude and Intention

Today I am grateful for:

.......................................................................................
.......................................................................................
.......................................................................................
.......................................................................................
.......................................................................................
.......................................................................................
.......................................................................................
.......................................................................................
.......................................................................................
.......................................................................................
.......................................................................................
.......................................................................................

Today's challenge and how it serves me to achieve my Life Priorities.

.......................................................................................
.......................................................................................
.......................................................................................
.......................................................................................
.......................................................................................

My highest Intentions for Tomorrow:

.......................................................................................
.......................................................................................
.......................................................................................
.......................................................................................
.......................................................................................

# MAR 19

## Daily Gratitude and Intention

Today I am grateful for:

........................................................................................................................
........................................................................................................................
........................................................................................................................
........................................................................................................................
........................................................................................................................
........................................................................................................................
........................................................................................................................
........................................................................................................................
........................................................................................................................
........................................................................................................................
........................................................................................................................
........................................................................................................................
........................................................................................................................

Today's challenge and how it serves me to achieve my Life Priorities.

........................................................................................................................
........................................................................................................................
........................................................................................................................
........................................................................................................................
........................................................................................................................
........................................................................................................................

My highest Intentions for Tomorrow:

........................................................................................................................
........................................................................................................................
........................................................................................................................
........................................................................................................................
........................................................................................................................

*Gratitude can transform common days into thanksgivings, turn routine jobs into joy, and change ordinary opportunities into blessings.*
*— William Arthur Ward*

## Daily Gratitude and Intention

Today I am grateful for:

..................................................................................................
..................................................................................................
..................................................................................................
..................................................................................................
..................................................................................................
..................................................................................................
..................................................................................................
..................................................................................................
..................................................................................................
..................................................................................................
..................................................................................................

Today's challenge and how it serves me to achieve my Life Priorities.

..................................................................................................
..................................................................................................
..................................................................................................
..................................................................................................
..................................................................................................

My highest Intentions for Tomorrow:

..................................................................................................
..................................................................................................
..................................................................................................
..................................................................................................
..................................................................................................

# MAR 21

## Daily Gratitude and Intention

Today I am grateful for:

.................................................................................................................
.................................................................................................................
.................................................................................................................
.................................................................................................................
.................................................................................................................
.................................................................................................................
.................................................................................................................
.................................................................................................................
.................................................................................................................
.................................................................................................................
.................................................................................................................
.................................................................................................................

Today's challenge and how it serves me to achieve my Life Priorities.

.................................................................................................................
.................................................................................................................
.................................................................................................................
.................................................................................................................
.................................................................................................................

My highest Intentions for Tomorrow:

.................................................................................................................
.................................................................................................................
.................................................................................................................
.................................................................................................................
.................................................................................................................

## Daily Gratitude and Intention

Today I am grateful for:

............................................................................................

............................................................................................

............................................................................................

............................................................................................

............................................................................................

............................................................................................

............................................................................................

............................................................................................

............................................................................................

............................................................................................

............................................................................................

............................................................................................

............................................................................................

............................................................................................

**Today's challenge** and how it serves me to achieve my Life Priorities.

............................................................................................

............................................................................................

............................................................................................

............................................................................................

............................................................................................

My **highest Intentions** for Tomorrow:

............................................................................................

............................................................................................

............................................................................................

............................................................................................

............................................................................................

# MAR 23

*Gratitude consists of being more aware of what you have, than what you don't. — Anonymous*

## Daily Gratitude and Intention

Today I am grateful for:

..................................................................................................
..................................................................................................
..................................................................................................
..................................................................................................
..................................................................................................
..................................................................................................
..................................................................................................
..................................................................................................
..................................................................................................
..................................................................................................
..................................................................................................
..................................................................................................
..................................................................................................
..................................................................................................

Today's challenge and how it serves me to achieve my Life Priorities.

..................................................................................................
..................................................................................................
..................................................................................................
..................................................................................................
..................................................................................................

My highest Intentions for Tomorrow:

..................................................................................................
..................................................................................................
..................................................................................................
..................................................................................................
..................................................................................................

## Daily Gratitude and Intention

Today I am grateful for:

..............................................................................................................
..............................................................................................................
..............................................................................................................
..............................................................................................................
..............................................................................................................
..............................................................................................................
..............................................................................................................
..............................................................................................................
..............................................................................................................
..............................................................................................................
..............................................................................................................
..............................................................................................................
..............................................................................................................

Today's challenge and how it serves me to achieve my Life Priorities.

..............................................................................................................
..............................................................................................................
..............................................................................................................
..............................................................................................................
..............................................................................................................
..............................................................................................................

My highest Intentions for Tomorrow:

..............................................................................................................
..............................................................................................................
..............................................................................................................
..............................................................................................................
..............................................................................................................

# MAR 25

*Gratitude helps you to grow and expand; gratitude brings joy and laughter into your life and into the lives of all those around you. — Eileen Caddy*

## Daily Gratitude and Intention

Today I am grateful for:

........................................................................................................................
........................................................................................................................
........................................................................................................................
........................................................................................................................
........................................................................................................................
........................................................................................................................
........................................................................................................................
........................................................................................................................
........................................................................................................................
........................................................................................................................
........................................................................................................................
........................................................................................................................

Today's challenge and how it serves me to achieve my Life Priorities.

........................................................................................................................
........................................................................................................................
........................................................................................................................
........................................................................................................................
........................................................................................................................

My highest Intentions for Tomorrow:

........................................................................................................................
........................................................................................................................
........................................................................................................................
........................................................................................................................
........................................................................................................................

## Daily Gratitude and Intention

Today I am grateful for:

........................................................................................................................

........................................................................................................................

........................................................................................................................

........................................................................................................................

........................................................................................................................

........................................................................................................................

........................................................................................................................

........................................................................................................................

........................................................................................................................

........................................................................................................................

........................................................................................................................

........................................................................................................................

........................................................................................................................

Today's challenge and how it serves me to achieve my Life Priorities.

........................................................................................................................

........................................................................................................................

........................................................................................................................

........................................................................................................................

........................................................................................................................

........................................................................................................................

My highest Intentions for Tomorrow:

........................................................................................................................

........................................................................................................................

........................................................................................................................

........................................................................................................................

........................................................................................................................

........................................................................................................................

# MAR 27

## Daily Gratitude and Intention

Today I am grateful for:

.............................................................................................................

.............................................................................................................

.............................................................................................................

.............................................................................................................

.............................................................................................................

.............................................................................................................

.............................................................................................................

.............................................................................................................

.............................................................................................................

.............................................................................................................

.............................................................................................................

.............................................................................................................

Today's challenge and how it serves me to achieve my Life Priorities.

.............................................................................................................

.............................................................................................................

.............................................................................................................

.............................................................................................................

.............................................................................................................

My highest Intentions for Tomorrow:

.............................................................................................................

.............................................................................................................

.............................................................................................................

.............................................................................................................

*Gratitude is a twofold love — love coming to visit us, and love running out to greet a welcome guest.*
*— Henry Van Dyke*

## Daily Gratitude and Intention

Today I am grateful for:

......................................................................................................
......................................................................................................
......................................................................................................
......................................................................................................
......................................................................................................
......................................................................................................
......................................................................................................
......................................................................................................
......................................................................................................
......................................................................................................
......................................................................................................
......................................................................................................
......................................................................................................
......................................................................................................

Today's challenge and how it serves me to achieve my Life Priorities.

......................................................................................................
......................................................................................................
......................................................................................................
......................................................................................................
......................................................................................................

My highest Intentions for Tomorrow:

......................................................................................................
......................................................................................................
......................................................................................................
......................................................................................................
......................................................................................................

# MAR 29

## Daily Gratitude and Intention

Today I am grateful for:

.............................................................................................................................

.............................................................................................................................

.............................................................................................................................

.............................................................................................................................

.............................................................................................................................

.............................................................................................................................

.............................................................................................................................

.............................................................................................................................

.............................................................................................................................

.............................................................................................................................

.............................................................................................................................

.............................................................................................................................

.............................................................................................................................

Today's challenge and how it serves me to achieve my Life Priorities.

.............................................................................................................................

.............................................................................................................................

.............................................................................................................................

.............................................................................................................................

.............................................................................................................................

My highest Intentions for Tomorrow:

.............................................................................................................................

.............................................................................................................................

.............................................................................................................................

.............................................................................................................................

.............................................................................................................................

*Gratitude is an art of painting an adversity into a lovely picture. — Kak Sri*

# Daily Gratitude and Intention

Today I am grateful for:

...................................................................................................................................

...................................................................................................................................

...................................................................................................................................

...................................................................................................................................

...................................................................................................................................

...................................................................................................................................

...................................................................................................................................

...................................................................................................................................

...................................................................................................................................

...................................................................................................................................

...................................................................................................................................

...................................................................................................................................

Today's challenge and how it serves me to achieve my Life Priorities.

...................................................................................................................................

...................................................................................................................................

...................................................................................................................................

...................................................................................................................................

...................................................................................................................................

My highest Intentions for Tomorrow:

...................................................................................................................................

...................................................................................................................................

...................................................................................................................................

...................................................................................................................................

...................................................................................................................................

# MAR 31

## Daily Gratitude and Intention

Today I am grateful for:

..................................................................................................................................
..................................................................................................................................
..................................................................................................................................
..................................................................................................................................
..................................................................................................................................
..................................................................................................................................
..................................................................................................................................
..................................................................................................................................
..................................................................................................................................
..................................................................................................................................
..................................................................................................................................

Today's challenge and how it serves me to achieve my Life Priorities.

..................................................................................................................................
..................................................................................................................................
..................................................................................................................................
..................................................................................................................................
..................................................................................................................................

My highest Intentions for Tomorrow:

..................................................................................................................................
..................................................................................................................................
..................................................................................................................................
..................................................................................................................................
..................................................................................................................................

Thinking: the talking
of the soul with itself.

— Plato

# APRIL

## Monthly Intention Plan

Write the top priorities you intend to focus on in each area of your life during this month.

SPIRITUAL

..................................................................................................................
..................................................................................................................
..................................................................................................................
..................................................................................................................
..................................................................................................................
..................................................................................................................
..................................................................................................................

MENTAL / EDUCATION

..................................................................................................................
..................................................................................................................
..................................................................................................................
..................................................................................................................
..................................................................................................................
..................................................................................................................
..................................................................................................................
..................................................................................................................
..................................................................................................................

VOCATIONAL / CAREER

..................................................................................................................
..................................................................................................................
..................................................................................................................
..................................................................................................................
..................................................................................................................
..................................................................................................................
..................................................................................................................

## FINANCIAL / SAVING & INVESTING

.............................................................................................................................

.............................................................................................................................

.............................................................................................................................

.............................................................................................................................

.............................................................................................................................

.............................................................................................................................

.............................................................................................................................

## FAMILIAL / RELATIONSHIP

.............................................................................................................................

.............................................................................................................................

.............................................................................................................................

.............................................................................................................................

.............................................................................................................................

.............................................................................................................................

.............................................................................................................................

.............................................................................................................................

## SOCIAL / FRIENDS

.............................................................................................................................

.............................................................................................................................

.............................................................................................................................

.............................................................................................................................

.............................................................................................................................

.............................................................................................................................

.............................................................................................................................

.............................................................................................................................

## HEALTH & PHYSICAL APPEARANCE

.............................................................................................................................

.............................................................................................................................

.............................................................................................................................

.............................................................................................................................

.............................................................................................................................

.............................................................................................................................

.............................................................................................................................

*Gratitude is heaven itself. — William Blake*

## Daily Gratitude and Intention

Today I am grateful for:

..........................................................................
..........................................................................
..........................................................................
..........................................................................
..........................................................................
..........................................................................
..........................................................................
..........................................................................
..........................................................................
..........................................................................
..........................................................................
..........................................................................
..........................................................................

Today's challenge and how it serves me to achieve my Life Priorities.

..........................................................................
..........................................................................
..........................................................................
..........................................................................
..........................................................................
..........................................................................

My highest Intentions for Tomorrow:

..........................................................................
..........................................................................
..........................................................................
..........................................................................
..........................................................................

*Gratitude is medicine for a heart devastated by tragedy.*
*If you can only be thankful for the blue sky, then do so.*
*— Richelle E. Goodrich*

# Daily Gratitude and Intention

Today I am grateful for:

........................................................................................................................................
........................................................................................................................................
........................................................................................................................................
........................................................................................................................................
........................................................................................................................................
........................................................................................................................................
........................................................................................................................................
........................................................................................................................................
........................................................................................................................................
........................................................................................................................................
........................................................................................................................................
........................................................................................................................................

Today's challenge and how it serves me to achieve my Life Priorities.

........................................................................................................................................
........................................................................................................................................
........................................................................................................................................
........................................................................................................................................
........................................................................................................................................

My highest Intentions for Tomorrow:

........................................................................................................................................
........................................................................................................................................
........................................................................................................................................
........................................................................................................................................
........................................................................................................................................

*Gratitude is not only the greatest of virtues, but the parent of all others. — Marcus Tullius Cicero*

## Daily Gratitude and Intention

Today I am grateful for:

.............................................................................................................
.............................................................................................................
.............................................................................................................
.............................................................................................................
.............................................................................................................
.............................................................................................................
.............................................................................................................
.............................................................................................................
.............................................................................................................
.............................................................................................................
.............................................................................................................
.............................................................................................................
.............................................................................................................

Today's challenge and how it serves me to achieve my Life Priorities.

.............................................................................................................
.............................................................................................................
.............................................................................................................
.............................................................................................................
.............................................................................................................

My highest Intentions for Tomorrow:

.............................................................................................................
.............................................................................................................
.............................................................................................................
.............................................................................................................

*Gratitude is not only the memory but the homage of the heart rendered to God for his goodness. — Nathaniel Parker Willis*

# Daily Gratitude and Intention

Today I am grateful for:

........................................................................................
........................................................................................
........................................................................................
........................................................................................
........................................................................................
........................................................................................
........................................................................................
........................................................................................
........................................................................................
........................................................................................
........................................................................................
........................................................................................

Today's challenge and how it serves me to achieve my Life Priorities.

........................................................................................
........................................................................................
........................................................................................
........................................................................................
........................................................................................

My highest Intentions for Tomorrow:

........................................................................................
........................................................................................
........................................................................................
........................................................................................
........................................................................................

*Gratitude is one of the least articulate of the emotions, especially when it is deep. — Felix Frankfurter*

## Daily Gratitude and Intention

Today I am grateful for:

....................................................................................................
....................................................................................................
....................................................................................................
....................................................................................................
....................................................................................................
....................................................................................................
....................................................................................................
....................................................................................................
....................................................................................................
....................................................................................................
....................................................................................................
....................................................................................................

Today's challenge and how it serves me to achieve my Life Priorities.

....................................................................................................
....................................................................................................
....................................................................................................
....................................................................................................
....................................................................................................

My highest Intentions for Tomorrow:

....................................................................................................
....................................................................................................
....................................................................................................
....................................................................................................
....................................................................................................

*Gratitude is one of the sweet shortcuts to finding peace of mind and happiness inside. No matter what is going on outside of us, there's always something we could be grateful for.*
*— Barry Neil Kaufman*

# Daily Gratitude and Intention

Today I am grateful for:

...........................................................................................................................................
...........................................................................................................................................
...........................................................................................................................................
...........................................................................................................................................
...........................................................................................................................................
...........................................................................................................................................
...........................................................................................................................................
...........................................................................................................................................
...........................................................................................................................................
...........................................................................................................................................
...........................................................................................................................................
...........................................................................................................................................
...........................................................................................................................................

Today's challenge and how it serves me to achieve my Life Priorities.

...........................................................................................................................................
...........................................................................................................................................
...........................................................................................................................................
...........................................................................................................................................
...........................................................................................................................................

My highest Intentions for Tomorrow:

...........................................................................................................................................
...........................................................................................................................................
...........................................................................................................................................
...........................................................................................................................................
...........................................................................................................................................

# APR 7

## Daily Gratitude and Intention

Today I am grateful for:

..........................................................................................................
..........................................................................................................
..........................................................................................................
..........................................................................................................
..........................................................................................................
..........................................................................................................
..........................................................................................................
..........................................................................................................
..........................................................................................................
..........................................................................................................
..........................................................................................................
..........................................................................................................

Today's challenge and how it serves me to achieve my Life Priorities.

..........................................................................................................
..........................................................................................................
..........................................................................................................
..........................................................................................................
..........................................................................................................

My highest Intentions for Tomorrow:

..........................................................................................................
..........................................................................................................
..........................................................................................................
..........................................................................................................
..........................................................................................................

*Gratitude is pure happiness. Happiness is pure perfection.*
*— Sri Chinmoy*

## Daily Gratitude and Intention

Today I am grateful for:

Today's challenge and how it serves me to achieve my Life Priorities.

My highest Intentions for Tomorrow:

*Gratitude is riches. Complaint is poverty. — Doris Day*

## Daily Gratitude and Intention

Today I am grateful for:

..................................................................................................
..................................................................................................
..................................................................................................
..................................................................................................
..................................................................................................
..................................................................................................
..................................................................................................
..................................................................................................
..................................................................................................
..................................................................................................
..................................................................................................
..................................................................................................
..................................................................................................
..................................................................................................

Today's challenge and how it serves me to achieve my Life Priorities.

..................................................................................................
..................................................................................................
..................................................................................................
..................................................................................................
..................................................................................................

My highest Intentions for Tomorrow:

..................................................................................................
..................................................................................................
..................................................................................................
..................................................................................................

*Gratitude is the ability to experience life as a gift.*
*It liberates us from the prison of self-preoccupation.*
*— John Ortberg*

# APR 10

## Daily Gratitude and Intention

Today I am grateful for:

........................................................................

........................................................................

........................................................................

........................................................................

........................................................................

........................................................................

........................................................................

........................................................................

........................................................................

........................................................................

........................................................................

........................................................................

Today's challenge and how it serves me to achieve my Life Priorities.

........................................................................

........................................................................

........................................................................

........................................................................

........................................................................

My highest Intentions for Tomorrow:

........................................................................

........................................................................

........................................................................

........................................................................

# APR 11

## Daily Gratitude and Intention

Today I am grateful for:

......................................................................................................................
......................................................................................................................
......................................................................................................................
......................................................................................................................
......................................................................................................................
......................................................................................................................
......................................................................................................................
......................................................................................................................
......................................................................................................................
......................................................................................................................
......................................................................................................................
......................................................................................................................
......................................................................................................................
......................................................................................................................

Today's challenge and how it serves me to achieve my Life Priorities.

......................................................................................................................
......................................................................................................................
......................................................................................................................
......................................................................................................................
......................................................................................................................

My highest Intentions for Tomorrow:

......................................................................................................................
......................................................................................................................
......................................................................................................................
......................................................................................................................
......................................................................................................................

*Gratitude is the creative force, the mother and father of love. It is in gratitude that real love exists. Love expands only when gratitude is there. — Sri Chinmoy*

## Daily Gratitude and Intention

Today I am grateful for:

........................................................................................................

........................................................................................................

........................................................................................................

........................................................................................................

........................................................................................................

........................................................................................................

........................................................................................................

........................................................................................................

........................................................................................................

........................................................................................................

........................................................................................................

........................................................................................................

Today's challenge and how it serves me to achieve my Life Priorities.

........................................................................................................

........................................................................................................

........................................................................................................

........................................................................................................

My highest Intentions for Tomorrow:

........................................................................................................

........................................................................................................

........................................................................................................

........................................................................................................

# APR 13

## Daily Gratitude and Intention

Today I am grateful for:

.......................................................................................................................................
.......................................................................................................................................
.......................................................................................................................................
.......................................................................................................................................
.......................................................................................................................................
.......................................................................................................................................
.......................................................................................................................................
.......................................................................................................................................
.......................................................................................................................................
.......................................................................................................................................
.......................................................................................................................................
.......................................................................................................................................
.......................................................................................................................................

Today's challenge and how it serves me to achieve my Life Priorities.

.......................................................................................................................................
.......................................................................................................................................
.......................................................................................................................................
.......................................................................................................................................
.......................................................................................................................................

My highest Intentions for Tomorrow:

.......................................................................................................................................
.......................................................................................................................................
.......................................................................................................................................
.......................................................................................................................................
.......................................................................................................................................

## Daily Gratitude and Intention

Today I am grateful for:

.............................................................................................................................
.............................................................................................................................
.............................................................................................................................
.............................................................................................................................
.............................................................................................................................
.............................................................................................................................
.............................................................................................................................
.............................................................................................................................
.............................................................................................................................
.............................................................................................................................
.............................................................................................................................
.............................................................................................................................

Today's challenge and how it serves me to achieve my Life Priorities.

.............................................................................................................................
.............................................................................................................................
.............................................................................................................................
.............................................................................................................................
.............................................................................................................................

My highest Intentions for Tomorrow:

.............................................................................................................................
.............................................................................................................................
.............................................................................................................................
.............................................................................................................................
.............................................................................................................................

# APR 15

*Gratitude is the inward feeling of kindness received. Thankfulness is the natural impulse to express that feeling. Thanksgiving is the following of that impulse.*
*— Henry Van Dyke*

## Daily Gratitude and Intention

Today I am grateful for:

...........................................................................................................................
...........................................................................................................................
...........................................................................................................................
...........................................................................................................................
...........................................................................................................................
...........................................................................................................................
...........................................................................................................................
...........................................................................................................................
...........................................................................................................................
...........................................................................................................................
...........................................................................................................................
...........................................................................................................................
...........................................................................................................................
...........................................................................................................................

Today's challenge and how it serves me to achieve my Life Priorities.

...........................................................................................................................
...........................................................................................................................
...........................................................................................................................
...........................................................................................................................
...........................................................................................................................
...........................................................................................................................

My highest Intentions for Tomorrow:

...........................................................................................................................
...........................................................................................................................
...........................................................................................................................
...........................................................................................................................
...........................................................................................................................
...........................................................................................................................

*Gratitude is the least of the virtues, but ingratitude is the worst of vices. — Thomas Fuller*

## Daily Gratitude and Intention

Today I am grateful for:

........................................................................................................

........................................................................................................

........................................................................................................

........................................................................................................

........................................................................................................

........................................................................................................

........................................................................................................

........................................................................................................

........................................................................................................

........................................................................................................

........................................................................................................

........................................................................................................

........................................................................................................

Today's challenge and how it serves me to achieve my Life Priorities.

........................................................................................................

........................................................................................................

........................................................................................................

........................................................................................................

........................................................................................................

My highest Intentions for Tomorrow:

........................................................................................................

........................................................................................................

........................................................................................................

........................................................................................................

........................................................................................................

*Gratitude is the memory of the heart.*
*— Jean Baptiste Massieu*

## Daily Gratitude and Intention

Today I am grateful for:

..................................................................................................
..................................................................................................
..................................................................................................
..................................................................................................
..................................................................................................
..................................................................................................
..................................................................................................
..................................................................................................
..................................................................................................
..................................................................................................
..................................................................................................
..................................................................................................
..................................................................................................

Today's challenge and how it serves me to achieve my Life Priorities.

..................................................................................................
..................................................................................................
..................................................................................................
..................................................................................................
..................................................................................................

My highest Intentions for Tomorrow:

..................................................................................................
..................................................................................................
..................................................................................................
..................................................................................................
..................................................................................................

*Gratitude is the most exquisite form of courtesy.*
*— Jacques Maritain*

## Daily Gratitude and Intention

Today I am grateful for:

.....................................................................................................................................................................
.....................................................................................................................................................................
.....................................................................................................................................................................
.....................................................................................................................................................................
.....................................................................................................................................................................
.....................................................................................................................................................................
.....................................................................................................................................................................
.....................................................................................................................................................................
.....................................................................................................................................................................
.....................................................................................................................................................................
.....................................................................................................................................................................
.....................................................................................................................................................................
.....................................................................................................................................................................

Today's challenge and how it serves me to achieve my Life Priorities.

.....................................................................................................................................................................
.....................................................................................................................................................................
.....................................................................................................................................................................
.....................................................................................................................................................................
.....................................................................................................................................................................

My highest Intentions for Tomorrow:

.....................................................................................................................................................................
.....................................................................................................................................................................
.....................................................................................................................................................................
.....................................................................................................................................................................
.....................................................................................................................................................................

# APR 19

## Daily Gratitude and Intention

Today I am grateful for:

....................................................................................
....................................................................................
....................................................................................
....................................................................................
....................................................................................
....................................................................................
....................................................................................
....................................................................................
....................................................................................
....................................................................................
....................................................................................
....................................................................................
....................................................................................
....................................................................................

Today's challenge and how it serves me to achieve my Life Priorities.

....................................................................................
....................................................................................
....................................................................................
....................................................................................
....................................................................................

My highest Intentions for Tomorrow:

....................................................................................
....................................................................................
....................................................................................
....................................................................................
....................................................................................

## Daily Gratitude and Intention

Today I am grateful for:

..................................................................................................................
..................................................................................................................
..................................................................................................................
..................................................................................................................
..................................................................................................................
..................................................................................................................
..................................................................................................................
..................................................................................................................
..................................................................................................................
..................................................................................................................
..................................................................................................................
..................................................................................................................
..................................................................................................................

Today's challenge and how it serves me to achieve my Life Priorities.

..................................................................................................................
..................................................................................................................
..................................................................................................................
..................................................................................................................
..................................................................................................................

My highest Intentions for Tomorrow:

..................................................................................................................
..................................................................................................................
..................................................................................................................
..................................................................................................................
..................................................................................................................

# APR 21

## Daily Gratitude and Intention

Today I am grateful for:

.......................................................................................................
.......................................................................................................
.......................................................................................................
.......................................................................................................
.......................................................................................................
.......................................................................................................
.......................................................................................................
.......................................................................................................
.......................................................................................................
.......................................................................................................
.......................................................................................................
.......................................................................................................
.......................................................................................................

Today's challenge and how it serves me to achieve my Life Priorities.

.......................................................................................................
.......................................................................................................
.......................................................................................................
.......................................................................................................
.......................................................................................................

My highest Intentions for Tomorrow:

.......................................................................................................
.......................................................................................................
.......................................................................................................
.......................................................................................................
.......................................................................................................

Gratitude is the state of mind of thankfulness. As it is cultivated, we experience an increase in our "sympathetic joy," our happiness at another's happiness.
— Stephen Levine

# APR 22

## Daily Gratitude and Intention

Today I am grateful for:

.................................................................................................................................
.................................................................................................................................
.................................................................................................................................
.................................................................................................................................
.................................................................................................................................
.................................................................................................................................
.................................................................................................................................
.................................................................................................................................
.................................................................................................................................
.................................................................................................................................
.................................................................................................................................
.................................................................................................................................
.................................................................................................................................

Today's challenge and how it serves me to achieve my Life Priorities.

.................................................................................................................................
.................................................................................................................................
.................................................................................................................................
.................................................................................................................................
.................................................................................................................................

My highest Intentions for Tomorrow:

.................................................................................................................................
.................................................................................................................................
.................................................................................................................................
.................................................................................................................................
.................................................................................................................................

# APR 23

*Gratitude is the sweetest thing in a seeker's life—in all human life. If there is gratitude in your heart, then there will be tremendous sweetness in your eyes. — Sri Chinmoy*

## Daily Gratitude and Intention

Today I am grateful for:

........................................................................................
........................................................................................
........................................................................................
........................................................................................
........................................................................................
........................................................................................
........................................................................................
........................................................................................
........................................................................................
........................................................................................
........................................................................................
........................................................................................

Today's challenge and how it serves me to achieve my Life Priorities.

........................................................................................
........................................................................................
........................................................................................
........................................................................................
........................................................................................

My highest Intentions for Tomorrow:

........................................................................................
........................................................................................
........................................................................................
........................................................................................
........................................................................................

*Gratitude is the energy of faith.*

# Daily Gratitude and Intention

Today I am grateful for:

.......................................................................................................
.......................................................................................................
.......................................................................................................
.......................................................................................................
.......................................................................................................
.......................................................................................................
.......................................................................................................
.......................................................................................................
.......................................................................................................
.......................................................................................................
.......................................................................................................
.......................................................................................................
.......................................................................................................

Today's challenge and how it serves me to achieve my Life Priorities.

.......................................................................................................
.......................................................................................................
.......................................................................................................
.......................................................................................................
.......................................................................................................

My highest Intentions for Tomorrow:

.......................................................................................................
.......................................................................................................
.......................................................................................................
.......................................................................................................

# APR 25

## Daily Gratitude and Intention

Today I am grateful for:

.............................................................................
.............................................................................
.............................................................................
.............................................................................
.............................................................................
.............................................................................
.............................................................................
.............................................................................
.............................................................................
.............................................................................
.............................................................................
.............................................................................
.............................................................................

Today's challenge and how it serves me to achieve my Life Priorities.

.............................................................................
.............................................................................
.............................................................................
.............................................................................
.............................................................................

My highest Intentions for Tomorrow:

.............................................................................
.............................................................................
.............................................................................
.............................................................................
.............................................................................

*Gratitude isn't a burdening emotion. — Loretta Young*

# Daily Gratitude and Intention

Today I am grateful for:

.................................................................................................................................
.................................................................................................................................
.................................................................................................................................
.................................................................................................................................
.................................................................................................................................
.................................................................................................................................
.................................................................................................................................
.................................................................................................................................
.................................................................................................................................
.................................................................................................................................
.................................................................................................................................
.................................................................................................................................
.................................................................................................................................
.................................................................................................................................

Today's challenge and how it serves me to achieve my Life Priorities.

.................................................................................................................................
.................................................................................................................................
.................................................................................................................................
.................................................................................................................................
.................................................................................................................................
.................................................................................................................................

My highest Intentions for Tomorrow:

.................................................................................................................................
.................................................................................................................................
.................................................................................................................................
.................................................................................................................................
.................................................................................................................................

*Gratitude makes sense of our past, brings peace for today, and creates a vision for tomorrow.*
*— Melody Beattie*

## Daily Gratitude and Intention

Today I am grateful for:

.............................................................................................................................
.............................................................................................................................
.............................................................................................................................
.............................................................................................................................
.............................................................................................................................
.............................................................................................................................
.............................................................................................................................
.............................................................................................................................
.............................................................................................................................
.............................................................................................................................
.............................................................................................................................
.............................................................................................................................
.............................................................................................................................

Today's challenge and how it serves me to achieve my Life Priorities.

.............................................................................................................................
.............................................................................................................................
.............................................................................................................................
.............................................................................................................................
.............................................................................................................................
.............................................................................................................................

My highest Intentions for Tomorrow:

.............................................................................................................................
.............................................................................................................................
.............................................................................................................................
.............................................................................................................................
.............................................................................................................................

*Gratitude means to recognize the good in your life, be thankful for whatever you have; some people may not even have one of those things you consider precious to you (love, family, friends etc). Each day give thanks for the gift of life. You are blessed. — Pablo*

# APR 28

## Daily Gratitude and Intention

Today I am grateful for:

.................................................................................................................
.................................................................................................................
.................................................................................................................
.................................................................................................................
.................................................................................................................
.................................................................................................................
.................................................................................................................
.................................................................................................................
.................................................................................................................
.................................................................................................................
.................................................................................................................
.................................................................................................................
.................................................................................................................

Today's challenge and how it serves me to achieve my Life Priorities.

.................................................................................................................
.................................................................................................................
.................................................................................................................
.................................................................................................................
.................................................................................................................
.................................................................................................................

My highest Intentions for Tomorrow:

.................................................................................................................
.................................................................................................................
.................................................................................................................
.................................................................................................................
.................................................................................................................

# APR 29

## Daily Gratitude and Intention

Today I am grateful for:

........................................................................................................

........................................................................................................

........................................................................................................

........................................................................................................

........................................................................................................

........................................................................................................

........................................................................................................

........................................................................................................

........................................................................................................

........................................................................................................

........................................................................................................

Today's challenge and how it serves me to achieve my Life Priorities.

........................................................................................................

........................................................................................................

........................................................................................................

........................................................................................................

........................................................................................................

My highest Intentions for Tomorrow:

........................................................................................................

........................................................................................................

........................................................................................................

........................................................................................................

## Daily Gratitude and Intention

Today I am grateful for:

.......................................................................................
.......................................................................................
.......................................................................................
.......................................................................................
.......................................................................................
.......................................................................................
.......................................................................................
.......................................................................................
.......................................................................................
.......................................................................................
.......................................................................................
.......................................................................................
.......................................................................................
.......................................................................................
.......................................................................................

Today's challenge and how it serves me to achieve my Life Priorities.

.......................................................................................
.......................................................................................
.......................................................................................
.......................................................................................
.......................................................................................
.......................................................................................

My highest Intentions for Tomorrow:

.......................................................................................
.......................................................................................
.......................................................................................
.......................................................................................
.......................................................................................

# MAY

## Monthly Intention Plan

Write the top priorities you intend to focus on in each area of your life during this month.

SPIRITUAL

........................................................................................................
........................................................................................................
........................................................................................................
........................................................................................................
........................................................................................................
........................................................................................................
........................................................................................................

MENTAL / EDUCATION

........................................................................................................
........................................................................................................
........................................................................................................
........................................................................................................
........................................................................................................
........................................................................................................
........................................................................................................

VOCATIONAL / CAREER

........................................................................................................
........................................................................................................
........................................................................................................
........................................................................................................
........................................................................................................
........................................................................................................
........................................................................................................

## FINANCIAL / SAVING & INVESTING

........................................................................................
........................................................................................
........................................................................................
........................................................................................
........................................................................................
........................................................................................
........................................................................................

## FAMILIAL / RELATIONSHIP

........................................................................................
........................................................................................
........................................................................................
........................................................................................
........................................................................................
........................................................................................
........................................................................................

## SOCIAL / FRIENDS

........................................................................................
........................................................................................
........................................................................................
........................................................................................
........................................................................................
........................................................................................
........................................................................................

## HEALTH & PHYSICAL APPEARANCE

........................................................................................
........................................................................................
........................................................................................
........................................................................................
........................................................................................
........................................................................................
........................................................................................

# MAY 1

## Daily Gratitude and Intention

Today I am grateful for:

.......................................................................................................

.......................................................................................................

.......................................................................................................

.......................................................................................................

.......................................................................................................

.......................................................................................................

.......................................................................................................

.......................................................................................................

.......................................................................................................

.......................................................................................................

.......................................................................................................

.......................................................................................................

.......................................................................................................

.......................................................................................................

.......................................................................................................

Today's challenge and how it serves me to achieve my Life Priorities.

.......................................................................................................

.......................................................................................................

.......................................................................................................

.......................................................................................................

.......................................................................................................

My highest Intentions for Tomorrow:

.......................................................................................................

.......................................................................................................

.......................................................................................................

.......................................................................................................

.......................................................................................................

*Gratitude turns what we have into enough, and more. It turns denial into acceptance, chaos into order and confusion into clarity. — Melody Beattie*

# MAY 2

## Daily Gratitude and Intention

Today I am grateful for:

........................................................................................

........................................................................................

........................................................................................

........................................................................................

........................................................................................

........................................................................................

........................................................................................

........................................................................................

........................................................................................

........................................................................................

........................................................................................

........................................................................................

Today's challenge and how it serves me to achieve my Life Priorities.

........................................................................................

........................................................................................

........................................................................................

........................................................................................

........................................................................................

My highest Intentions for Tomorrow:

........................................................................................

........................................................................................

........................................................................................

........................................................................................

........................................................................................

# MAY 3

## Daily Gratitude and Intention

Today I am grateful for:

..................................................................................................
..................................................................................................
..................................................................................................
..................................................................................................
..................................................................................................
..................................................................................................
..................................................................................................
..................................................................................................
..................................................................................................
..................................................................................................
..................................................................................................
..................................................................................................
..................................................................................................

Today's challenge and how it serves me to achieve my Life Priorities.

..................................................................................................
..................................................................................................
..................................................................................................
..................................................................................................
..................................................................................................

My highest Intentions for Tomorrow:

..................................................................................................
..................................................................................................
..................................................................................................
..................................................................................................
..................................................................................................

## Daily Gratitude and Intention

Today I am grateful for:

........................................................................................

........................................................................................

........................................................................................

........................................................................................

........................................................................................

........................................................................................

........................................................................................

........................................................................................

........................................................................................

........................................................................................

........................................................................................

........................................................................................

........................................................................................

Today's challenge and how it serves me to achieve my Life Priorities.

........................................................................................

........................................................................................

........................................................................................

........................................................................................

........................................................................................

My highest Intentions for Tomorrow:

........................................................................................

........................................................................................

........................................................................................

........................................................................................

........................................................................................

# MAY 5

*He is a wise man who does not grieve for the things which he has not, but rejoices for those which he has.*
*— Epictetus*

## Daily Gratitude and Intention

Today I am grateful for:

........................................................................................................
........................................................................................................
........................................................................................................
........................................................................................................
........................................................................................................
........................................................................................................
........................................................................................................
........................................................................................................
........................................................................................................
........................................................................................................
........................................................................................................
........................................................................................................
........................................................................................................
........................................................................................................

Today's challenge and how it serves me to achieve my Life Priorities.

........................................................................................................
........................................................................................................
........................................................................................................
........................................................................................................
........................................................................................................

My highest Intentions for Tomorrow:

........................................................................................................
........................................................................................................
........................................................................................................
........................................................................................................

*He was aware of the value of the word of praise dropped at exactly the right moment; and he would have thought himself extremely stupid to withhold what cost him so little and was productive of such desirable results.*
*— Georgette Heyer, Sylvester*

# MAY 6

## Daily Gratitude and Intention

Today I am grateful for:

......................................................................................................
......................................................................................................
......................................................................................................
......................................................................................................
......................................................................................................
......................................................................................................
......................................................................................................
......................................................................................................
......................................................................................................
......................................................................................................
......................................................................................................
......................................................................................................

Today's challenge and how it serves me to achieve my Life Priorities.

......................................................................................................
......................................................................................................
......................................................................................................
......................................................................................................

My highest Intentions for Tomorrow:

......................................................................................................
......................................................................................................
......................................................................................................
......................................................................................................

# MAY 7

*He who thanks but with the lips thanks but in part; the full, the true Thanksgiving comes from the heart.* — J. A. Shedd

## Daily Gratitude and Intention

Today I am grateful for:

..................................................................................................................................

..................................................................................................................................

..................................................................................................................................

..................................................................................................................................

..................................................................................................................................

..................................................................................................................................

..................................................................................................................................

..................................................................................................................................

..................................................................................................................................

..................................................................................................................................

..................................................................................................................................

..................................................................................................................................

Today's challenge and how it serves me to achieve my Life Priorities.

..................................................................................................................................

..................................................................................................................................

..................................................................................................................................

..................................................................................................................................

..................................................................................................................................

My highest Intentions for Tomorrow:

..................................................................................................................................

..................................................................................................................................

..................................................................................................................................

..................................................................................................................................

..................................................................................................................................

*Hem your blessings with thankfulness so they don't unravel.*
*— Author Unknown*

## Daily Gratitude and Intention

Today I am grateful for:

.................................................................................................................................
.................................................................................................................................
.................................................................................................................................
.................................................................................................................................
.................................................................................................................................
.................................................................................................................................
.................................................................................................................................
.................................................................................................................................
.................................................................................................................................
.................................................................................................................................
.................................................................................................................................
.................................................................................................................................

Today's challenge and how it serves me to achieve my Life Priorities.

.................................................................................................................................
.................................................................................................................................
.................................................................................................................................
.................................................................................................................................
.................................................................................................................................

My highest Intentions for Tomorrow:

.................................................................................................................................
.................................................................................................................................
.................................................................................................................................
.................................................................................................................................
.................................................................................................................................

# MAY 9

## Daily Gratitude and Intention

Today I am grateful for:

...........................................................................................

...........................................................................................

...........................................................................................

...........................................................................................

...........................................................................................

...........................................................................................

...........................................................................................

...........................................................................................

...........................................................................................

...........................................................................................

...........................................................................................

...........................................................................................

Today's challenge and how it serves me to achieve my Life Priorities.

...........................................................................................

...........................................................................................

...........................................................................................

...........................................................................................

...........................................................................................

...........................................................................................

My highest Intentions for Tomorrow:

...........................................................................................

...........................................................................................

...........................................................................................

...........................................................................................

...........................................................................................

# MAY 10

## Daily Gratitude and Intention

Today I am grateful for:

.........................................................................................................
.........................................................................................................
.........................................................................................................
.........................................................................................................
.........................................................................................................
.........................................................................................................
.........................................................................................................
.........................................................................................................
.........................................................................................................
.........................................................................................................
.........................................................................................................
.........................................................................................................
.........................................................................................................
.........................................................................................................

Today's challenge and how it serves me to achieve my Life Priorities.

.........................................................................................................
.........................................................................................................
.........................................................................................................
.........................................................................................................
.........................................................................................................

My highest Intentions for Tomorrow:

.........................................................................................................
.........................................................................................................
.........................................................................................................
.........................................................................................................
.........................................................................................................

# MAY 11

## Daily Gratitude and Intention

Today I am grateful for:

.............................................................................................
.............................................................................................
.............................................................................................
.............................................................................................
.............................................................................................
.............................................................................................
.............................................................................................
.............................................................................................
.............................................................................................
.............................................................................................
.............................................................................................
.............................................................................................
.............................................................................................

Today's challenge and how it serves me to achieve my Life Priorities.

.............................................................................................
.............................................................................................
.............................................................................................
.............................................................................................
.............................................................................................

My highest Intentions for Tomorrow:

.............................................................................................
.............................................................................................
.............................................................................................
.............................................................................................
.............................................................................................

## Daily Gratitude and Intention

Today I am grateful for:

..........................................................................................................
..........................................................................................................
..........................................................................................................
..........................................................................................................
..........................................................................................................
..........................................................................................................
..........................................................................................................
..........................................................................................................
..........................................................................................................
..........................................................................................................
..........................................................................................................
..........................................................................................................
..........................................................................................................

Today's challenge and how it serves me to achieve my Life Priorities.

..........................................................................................................
..........................................................................................................
..........................................................................................................
..........................................................................................................
..........................................................................................................

My highest Intentions for Tomorrow:

..........................................................................................................
..........................................................................................................
..........................................................................................................
..........................................................................................................
..........................................................................................................

# MAY 13

## Daily Gratitude and Intention

Today I am grateful for:

.............................................................................

.............................................................................

.............................................................................

.............................................................................

.............................................................................

.............................................................................

.............................................................................

.............................................................................

.............................................................................

.............................................................................

.............................................................................

.............................................................................

Today's challenge and how it serves me to achieve my Life Priorities.

.............................................................................

.............................................................................

.............................................................................

.............................................................................

.............................................................................

My highest Intentions for Tomorrow:

.............................................................................

.............................................................................

.............................................................................

.............................................................................

.............................................................................

*I am so grateful for gratitude, a magical magnet.*
*A natural expression of a loving heart, The*
*power of gratitude recharges our souls.*
*— Katherine Scherer and Eileen Bodoh*

## Daily Gratitude and Intention

Today I am grateful for:

......................................................................................................................
......................................................................................................................
......................................................................................................................
......................................................................................................................
......................................................................................................................
......................................................................................................................
......................................................................................................................
......................................................................................................................
......................................................................................................................
......................................................................................................................
......................................................................................................................
......................................................................................................................

Today's challenge and how it serves me to achieve my Life Priorities.

......................................................................................................................
......................................................................................................................
......................................................................................................................
......................................................................................................................
......................................................................................................................

My highest Intentions for Tomorrow:

......................................................................................................................
......................................................................................................................
......................................................................................................................
......................................................................................................................
......................................................................................................................

# MAY 15

I am thankful, that sometimes I am the black sky for your stars to shine against. I am the desert where your oasis lives. I am the thorn where your rose blossoms. I am the oyster where your pearl form. I am the mine where your diamond will shape.
— Avantika

## Daily Gratitude and Intention

Today I am grateful for:

.......................................................................................................................................
.......................................................................................................................................
.......................................................................................................................................
.......................................................................................................................................
.......................................................................................................................................
.......................................................................................................................................
.......................................................................................................................................
.......................................................................................................................................
.......................................................................................................................................
.......................................................................................................................................
.......................................................................................................................................
.......................................................................................................................................
.......................................................................................................................................

Today's challenge and how it serves me to achieve my Life Priorities.

.......................................................................................................................................
.......................................................................................................................................
.......................................................................................................................................
.......................................................................................................................................
.......................................................................................................................................

My highest Intentions for Tomorrow:

.......................................................................................................................................
.......................................................................................................................................
.......................................................................................................................................
.......................................................................................................................................

*I awoke this morning with devout thanksgiving for my friends, the old and the new.*
*— Ralph Waldo Emerson*

# MAY 16

## Daily Gratitude and Intention

Today I am grateful for:

.................................................................................................
.................................................................................................
.................................................................................................
.................................................................................................
.................................................................................................
.................................................................................................
.................................................................................................
.................................................................................................
.................................................................................................
.................................................................................................
.................................................................................................
.................................................................................................
.................................................................................................

Today's challenge and how it serves me to achieve my Life Priorities.

.................................................................................................
.................................................................................................
.................................................................................................
.................................................................................................
.................................................................................................

My highest Intentions for Tomorrow:

.................................................................................................
.................................................................................................
.................................................................................................
.................................................................................................
.................................................................................................

# MAY 17

## Daily Gratitude and Intention

Today I am grateful for:

.................................................................................................
.................................................................................................
.................................................................................................
.................................................................................................
.................................................................................................
.................................................................................................
.................................................................................................
.................................................................................................
.................................................................................................
.................................................................................................
.................................................................................................
.................................................................................................
.................................................................................................
.................................................................................................

Today's challenge and how it serves me to achieve my Life Priorities.

.................................................................................................
.................................................................................................
.................................................................................................
.................................................................................................
.................................................................................................

My highest Intentions for Tomorrow:

.................................................................................................
.................................................................................................
.................................................................................................
.................................................................................................
.................................................................................................

## Daily Gratitude and Intention

Today I am grateful for:

............................................................................
............................................................................
............................................................................
............................................................................
............................................................................
............................................................................
............................................................................
............................................................................
............................................................................
............................................................................
............................................................................
............................................................................
............................................................................
............................................................................
............................................................................

Today's challenge and how it serves me to achieve my Life Priorities.

............................................................................
............................................................................
............................................................................
............................................................................
............................................................................

My highest Intentions for Tomorrow:

............................................................................
............................................................................
............................................................................
............................................................................
............................................................................

# MAY 19

## Daily Gratitude and Intention

Today I am grateful for:

........................................................................................................................

........................................................................................................................

........................................................................................................................

........................................................................................................................

........................................................................................................................

........................................................................................................................

........................................................................................................................

........................................................................................................................

........................................................................................................................

........................................................................................................................

........................................................................................................................

........................................................................................................................

Today's challenge and how it serves me to achieve my Life Priorities.

........................................................................................................................

........................................................................................................................

........................................................................................................................

........................................................................................................................

........................................................................................................................

My highest Intentions for Tomorrow:

........................................................................................................................

........................................................................................................................

........................................................................................................................

........................................................................................................................

I have found that it is not enough for me to be thankful. I have a desire to do something in return. To do thanks. To give thanks. Give things. Give thoughts. Give love. So gratitude becomes the gift, creating a cycle of giving and receiving, the endless waterfall. — Elizabeth Bartlett

## Daily Gratitude and Intention

Today I am grateful for:

.......................................................................................................................
.......................................................................................................................
.......................................................................................................................
.......................................................................................................................
.......................................................................................................................
.......................................................................................................................
.......................................................................................................................
.......................................................................................................................
.......................................................................................................................
.......................................................................................................................
.......................................................................................................................
.......................................................................................................................

Today's challenge and how it serves me to achieve my Life Priorities.

.......................................................................................................................
.......................................................................................................................
.......................................................................................................................
.......................................................................................................................
.......................................................................................................................

My highest Intentions for Tomorrow:

.......................................................................................................................
.......................................................................................................................
.......................................................................................................................
.......................................................................................................................
.......................................................................................................................

OptimumThinking.net

# MAY 21

*Only children and a few spiritually evolved people are born to feel gratitude as naturally as they breathe, without even thinking. Most of us come to it step by painful step, to discover that gratitude is a form of acceptance. — Faith Baldwin*

## Daily Gratitude and Intention

Today I am grateful for:

........................................................................................................
........................................................................................................
........................................................................................................
........................................................................................................
........................................................................................................
........................................................................................................
........................................................................................................
........................................................................................................
........................................................................................................
........................................................................................................
........................................................................................................
........................................................................................................

Today's challenge and how it serves me to achieve my Life Priorities.

........................................................................................................
........................................................................................................
........................................................................................................
........................................................................................................
........................................................................................................

My highest Intentions for Tomorrow:

........................................................................................................
........................................................................................................
........................................................................................................
........................................................................................................
........................................................................................................

*I have learned that in every circumstance that comes my way, I can choose to respond in one of two ways: I can whine or I can worship! And I can't worship without giving thanks. It just isn't possible.*
*— Nancy Leigh DeMoss*

# MAY 22

## Daily Gratitude and Intention

Today I am grateful for:

.................................................................................................................
.................................................................................................................
.................................................................................................................
.................................................................................................................
.................................................................................................................
.................................................................................................................
.................................................................................................................
.................................................................................................................
.................................................................................................................
.................................................................................................................
.................................................................................................................
.................................................................................................................

Today's challenge and how it serves me to achieve my Life Priorities.

.................................................................................................................
.................................................................................................................
.................................................................................................................
.................................................................................................................
.................................................................................................................

My highest Intentions for Tomorrow:

.................................................................................................................
.................................................................................................................
.................................................................................................................
.................................................................................................................
.................................................................................................................

# MAY 23

## Daily Gratitude and Intention

Today I am grateful for:

.................................................................................................
.................................................................................................
.................................................................................................
.................................................................................................
.................................................................................................
.................................................................................................
.................................................................................................
.................................................................................................
.................................................................................................
.................................................................................................
.................................................................................................
.................................................................................................
.................................................................................................
.................................................................................................

Today's challenge and how it serves me to achieve my Life Priorities.

.................................................................................................
.................................................................................................
.................................................................................................
.................................................................................................
.................................................................................................
.................................................................................................

My highest Intentions for Tomorrow:

.................................................................................................
.................................................................................................
.................................................................................................
.................................................................................................
.................................................................................................

*I see the glass half full and thank God for what I have.*
*— Ana Monnar*

## Daily Gratitude and Intention

Today I am grateful for:

.......................................................................................................
.......................................................................................................
.......................................................................................................
.......................................................................................................
.......................................................................................................
.......................................................................................................
.......................................................................................................
.......................................................................................................
.......................................................................................................
.......................................................................................................
.......................................................................................................
.......................................................................................................
.......................................................................................................

Today's challenge and how it serves me to achieve my Life Priorities.

.......................................................................................................
.......................................................................................................
.......................................................................................................
.......................................................................................................
.......................................................................................................
.......................................................................................................

My highest Intentions for Tomorrow:

.......................................................................................................
.......................................................................................................
.......................................................................................................
.......................................................................................................
.......................................................................................................

# MAY 25

## Daily Gratitude and Intention

Today I am grateful for:

..............................................................................................................
..............................................................................................................
..............................................................................................................
..............................................................................................................
..............................................................................................................
..............................................................................................................
..............................................................................................................
..............................................................................................................
..............................................................................................................
..............................................................................................................
..............................................................................................................
..............................................................................................................
..............................................................................................................
..............................................................................................................

Today's challenge and how it serves me to achieve my Life Priorities.

..............................................................................................................
..............................................................................................................
..............................................................................................................
..............................................................................................................
..............................................................................................................
..............................................................................................................

My highest Intentions for Tomorrow:

..............................................................................................................
..............................................................................................................
..............................................................................................................
..............................................................................................................
..............................................................................................................

# MAY 26

## Daily Gratitude and Intention

Today I am grateful for:

.................................................................................
.................................................................................
.................................................................................
.................................................................................
.................................................................................
.................................................................................
.................................................................................
.................................................................................
.................................................................................
.................................................................................
.................................................................................
.................................................................................

Today's challenge and how it serves me to achieve my Life Priorities.

.................................................................................
.................................................................................
.................................................................................
.................................................................................
.................................................................................

My highest Intentions for Tomorrow:

.................................................................................
.................................................................................
.................................................................................
.................................................................................
.................................................................................

**OptimumThinking.net**

# MAY 27

## Daily Gratitude and Intention

Today I am grateful for:

........................................................................

........................................................................

........................................................................

........................................................................

........................................................................

........................................................................

........................................................................

........................................................................

........................................................................

........................................................................

........................................................................

........................................................................

Today's challenge and how it serves me to achieve my Life Priorities.

........................................................................

........................................................................

........................................................................

........................................................................

........................................................................

My highest Intentions for Tomorrow:

........................................................................

........................................................................

........................................................................

........................................................................

........................................................................

*The world is so exquisite with so much love and moral depth, that there is no reason to deceive ourselves with pretty stories for which there's little good evidence. Far better it seems to me, in our vulnerability, is to look death in the eye and to be grateful every day for the brief but magnificent opportunity that life provides.*
*— Carl Sagan*

# MAY 28

## Daily Gratitude and Intention

Today I am grateful for:

..................................................................................................
..................................................................................................
..................................................................................................
..................................................................................................
..................................................................................................
..................................................................................................
..................................................................................................
..................................................................................................
..................................................................................................
..................................................................................................
..................................................................................................

Today's challenge and how it serves me to achieve my Life Priorities.

..................................................................................................
..................................................................................................
..................................................................................................
..................................................................................................
..................................................................................................

My highest Intentions for Tomorrow:

..................................................................................................
..................................................................................................
..................................................................................................
..................................................................................................
..................................................................................................

# MAY 29

*I would maintain that thanks are the highest form of thought; and that gratitude is happiness doubled by wonder. — G.K. Chesterton*

## Daily Gratitude and Intention

Today I am grateful for:

.......................................................................................................................................................
.......................................................................................................................................................
.......................................................................................................................................................
.......................................................................................................................................................
.......................................................................................................................................................
.......................................................................................................................................................
.......................................................................................................................................................
.......................................................................................................................................................
.......................................................................................................................................................
.......................................................................................................................................................
.......................................................................................................................................................
.......................................................................................................................................................
.......................................................................................................................................................
.......................................................................................................................................................

Today's challenge and how it serves me to achieve my Life Priorities.

.......................................................................................................................................................
.......................................................................................................................................................
.......................................................................................................................................................
.......................................................................................................................................................
.......................................................................................................................................................

My highest Intentions for Tomorrow:

.......................................................................................................................................................
.......................................................................................................................................................
.......................................................................................................................................................
.......................................................................................................................................................
.......................................................................................................................................................

*If a fellow isn't thankful for what he's got, he isn't likely to be thankful for what he's going to get. — Frank A. Clark*

# MAY 30

## Daily Gratitude and Intention

Today I am grateful for:

...........................................................................................................................................

...........................................................................................................................................

...........................................................................................................................................

...........................................................................................................................................

...........................................................................................................................................

...........................................................................................................................................

...........................................................................................................................................

...........................................................................................................................................

...........................................................................................................................................

...........................................................................................................................................

...........................................................................................................................................

...........................................................................................................................................

Today's challenge and how it serves me to achieve my Life Priorities.

...........................................................................................................................................

...........................................................................................................................................

...........................................................................................................................................

...........................................................................................................................................

...........................................................................................................................................

My highest Intentions for Tomorrow:

...........................................................................................................................................

...........................................................................................................................................

...........................................................................................................................................

...........................................................................................................................................

...........................................................................................................................................

# MAY 31

## Daily Gratitude and Intention

Today I am grateful for:

.......................................................................................................
.......................................................................................................
.......................................................................................................
.......................................................................................................
.......................................................................................................
.......................................................................................................
.......................................................................................................
.......................................................................................................
.......................................................................................................
.......................................................................................................
.......................................................................................................
.......................................................................................................

Today's challenge and how it serves me to achieve my Life Priorities.

.......................................................................................................
.......................................................................................................
.......................................................................................................
.......................................................................................................
.......................................................................................................

My highest Intentions for Tomorrow:

.......................................................................................................
.......................................................................................................
.......................................................................................................
.......................................................................................................
.......................................................................................................

The beautiful things in the world
cannot be seen or even touched —
they must be felt with the heart

— Hellen Keller

# JUNE

## Monthly Intention Plan

Write the top priorities you intend to focus on in each area of your life during this month.

SPIRITUAL

.............................................................................
.............................................................................
.............................................................................
.............................................................................
.............................................................................
.............................................................................
.............................................................................
.............................................................................

MENTAL / EDUCATION

.............................................................................
.............................................................................
.............................................................................
.............................................................................
.............................................................................
.............................................................................
.............................................................................
.............................................................................

VOCATIONAL / CAREER

.............................................................................
.............................................................................
.............................................................................
.............................................................................
.............................................................................
.............................................................................
.............................................................................
.............................................................................

## FINANCIAL / SAVING & INVESTING

........................................................................................................................................
........................................................................................................................................
........................................................................................................................................
........................................................................................................................................
........................................................................................................................................
........................................................................................................................................
........................................................................................................................................

## FAMILIAL / RELATIONSHIP

........................................................................................................................................
........................................................................................................................................
........................................................................................................................................
........................................................................................................................................
........................................................................................................................................
........................................................................................................................................
........................................................................................................................................
........................................................................................................................................

## SOCIAL / FRIENDS

........................................................................................................................................
........................................................................................................................................
........................................................................................................................................
........................................................................................................................................
........................................................................................................................................
........................................................................................................................................
........................................................................................................................................
........................................................................................................................................

## HEALTH & PHYSICAL APPEARANCE

........................................................................................................................................
........................................................................................................................................
........................................................................................................................................
........................................................................................................................................
........................................................................................................................................
........................................................................................................................................
........................................................................................................................................

# JUN 1

## Daily Gratitude and Intention

Today I am grateful for:

.......................................................................................................
.......................................................................................................
.......................................................................................................
.......................................................................................................
.......................................................................................................
.......................................................................................................
.......................................................................................................
.......................................................................................................
.......................................................................................................
.......................................................................................................
.......................................................................................................
.......................................................................................................

Today's challenge and how it serves me to achieve my Life Priorities.

.......................................................................................................
.......................................................................................................
.......................................................................................................
.......................................................................................................
.......................................................................................................
.......................................................................................................

My highest Intentions for Tomorrow:

.......................................................................................................
.......................................................................................................
.......................................................................................................
.......................................................................................................
.......................................................................................................
.......................................................................................................

*If people offer their help or wisdom as you go through life, accept it gratefully. You can learn much from those who have gone before you. — Edmund O'Neill*

## Daily Gratitude and Intention

Today I am grateful for:

..............................................................................................................
..............................................................................................................
..............................................................................................................
..............................................................................................................
..............................................................................................................
..............................................................................................................
..............................................................................................................
..............................................................................................................
..............................................................................................................
..............................................................................................................
..............................................................................................................
..............................................................................................................

Today's challenge and how it serves me to achieve my Life Priorities.

..............................................................................................................
..............................................................................................................
..............................................................................................................
..............................................................................................................
..............................................................................................................

My highest Intentions for Tomorrow:

..............................................................................................................
..............................................................................................................
..............................................................................................................
..............................................................................................................
..............................................................................................................

# JUN 3

## Daily Gratitude and Intention

Today I am grateful for:

...................................................................................................................
...................................................................................................................
...................................................................................................................
...................................................................................................................
...................................................................................................................
...................................................................................................................
...................................................................................................................
...................................................................................................................
...................................................................................................................
...................................................................................................................
...................................................................................................................
...................................................................................................................
...................................................................................................................

Today's challenge and how it serves me to achieve my Life Priorities.

...................................................................................................................
...................................................................................................................
...................................................................................................................
...................................................................................................................
...................................................................................................................

My highest Intentions for Tomorrow:

...................................................................................................................
...................................................................................................................
...................................................................................................................
...................................................................................................................
...................................................................................................................

*If the only prayer you said in your whole life was, "thank you," that would suffice.— Meister Eckhart*

## Daily Gratitude and Intention

Today I am grateful for:

......................................................................................................................................
......................................................................................................................................
......................................................................................................................................
......................................................................................................................................
......................................................................................................................................
......................................................................................................................................
......................................................................................................................................
......................................................................................................................................
......................................................................................................................................
......................................................................................................................................
......................................................................................................................................
......................................................................................................................................
......................................................................................................................................
......................................................................................................................................
......................................................................................................................................

Today's challenge and how it serves me to achieve my Life Priorities.

......................................................................................................................................
......................................................................................................................................
......................................................................................................................................
......................................................................................................................................
......................................................................................................................................

My highest Intentions for Tomorrow:

......................................................................................................................................
......................................................................................................................................
......................................................................................................................................
......................................................................................................................................
......................................................................................................................................

# JUN 5

*In order to complete our amazing life journey successfully, it is vital that we turn each and every dark tear into a pearl of wisdom, and find the blessing in every curse.*
*— Anthon St. Maarten*

## Daily Gratitude and Intention

Today I am grateful for:

.......................................................................................................................
.......................................................................................................................
.......................................................................................................................
.......................................................................................................................
.......................................................................................................................
.......................................................................................................................
.......................................................................................................................
.......................................................................................................................
.......................................................................................................................
.......................................................................................................................
.......................................................................................................................
.......................................................................................................................
.......................................................................................................................

Today's challenge and how it serves me to achieve my Life Priorities.

.......................................................................................................................
.......................................................................................................................
.......................................................................................................................
.......................................................................................................................
.......................................................................................................................
.......................................................................................................................

My highest Intentions for Tomorrow:

.......................................................................................................................
.......................................................................................................................
.......................................................................................................................
.......................................................................................................................
.......................................................................................................................

*If we want to keep the blessings of life coming to us,*
*we must learn to be grateful for whatever is given.*
*— Harold Klemp*

## Daily Gratitude and Intention

Today I am grateful for:

.......................................................................................................
.......................................................................................................
.......................................................................................................
.......................................................................................................
.......................................................................................................
.......................................................................................................
.......................................................................................................
.......................................................................................................
.......................................................................................................
.......................................................................................................
.......................................................................................................
.......................................................................................................
.......................................................................................................
.......................................................................................................
.......................................................................................................
.......................................................................................................

Today's challenge and how it serves me to achieve my Life Priorities.

.......................................................................................................
.......................................................................................................
.......................................................................................................
.......................................................................................................
.......................................................................................................

My highest Intentions for Tomorrow:

.......................................................................................................
.......................................................................................................
.......................................................................................................
.......................................................................................................
.......................................................................................................

# JUN 7

*If you always try to measure yourself with money...well, it's like counting backwards, the more you keep on, the less you'll have to show for it.*
*— Steven J. Carroll, The Road to Jericho*

## Daily Gratitude and Intention

Today I am grateful for:

.................................................................................................
.................................................................................................
.................................................................................................
.................................................................................................
.................................................................................................
.................................................................................................
.................................................................................................
.................................................................................................
.................................................................................................
.................................................................................................
.................................................................................................
.................................................................................................
.................................................................................................
.................................................................................................
.................................................................................................

Today's challenge and how it serves me to achieve my Life Priorities.

.................................................................................................
.................................................................................................
.................................................................................................
.................................................................................................
.................................................................................................

My highest Intentions for Tomorrow:

.................................................................................................
.................................................................................................
.................................................................................................
.................................................................................................
.................................................................................................

## Daily Gratitude and Intention

Today I am grateful for:

..................................................................................................................
..................................................................................................................
..................................................................................................................
..................................................................................................................
..................................................................................................................
..................................................................................................................
..................................................................................................................
..................................................................................................................
..................................................................................................................
..................................................................................................................
..................................................................................................................
..................................................................................................................
..................................................................................................................

Today's challenge and how it serves me to achieve my Life Priorities.

..................................................................................................................
..................................................................................................................
..................................................................................................................
..................................................................................................................
..................................................................................................................

My highest Intentions for Tomorrow:

..................................................................................................................
..................................................................................................................
..................................................................................................................
..................................................................................................................
..................................................................................................................

# JUN 9

*If you concentrate on finding whatever is good in every situation, you will discover that your life will suddenly be filled with gratitude, a feeling that nurtures the soul.*
— Rabbi Harold Kushner

## Daily Gratitude and Intention

Today I am grateful for:

..............................................................................................................
..............................................................................................................
..............................................................................................................
..............................................................................................................
..............................................................................................................
..............................................................................................................
..............................................................................................................
..............................................................................................................
..............................................................................................................
..............................................................................................................
..............................................................................................................
..............................................................................................................

Today's challenge and how it serves me to achieve my Life Priorities.

..............................................................................................................
..............................................................................................................
..............................................................................................................
..............................................................................................................
..............................................................................................................

My highest Intentions for Tomorrow:

..............................................................................................................
..............................................................................................................
..............................................................................................................
..............................................................................................................
..............................................................................................................

*If you count all your assets, you always show a profit.*
*— Robert Quillen*

## Daily Gratitude and Intention

Today I am grateful for:

........................................................................................................

........................................................................................................

........................................................................................................

........................................................................................................

........................................................................................................

........................................................................................................

........................................................................................................

........................................................................................................

........................................................................................................

........................................................................................................

........................................................................................................

........................................................................................................

Today's challenge and how it serves me to achieve my Life Priorities.

........................................................................................................

........................................................................................................

........................................................................................................

........................................................................................................

........................................................................................................

My highest Intentions for Tomorrow:

........................................................................................................

........................................................................................................

........................................................................................................

........................................................................................................

........................................................................................................

# JUN 11

## Daily Gratitude and Intention

Today I am grateful for:

........................................................................................

........................................................................................

........................................................................................

........................................................................................

........................................................................................

........................................................................................

........................................................................................

........................................................................................

........................................................................................

........................................................................................

........................................................................................

........................................................................................

Today's challenge and how it serves me to achieve my Life Priorities.

........................................................................................

........................................................................................

........................................................................................

........................................................................................

........................................................................................

My highest Intentions for Tomorrow:

........................................................................................

........................................................................................

........................................................................................

........................................................................................

........................................................................................

## Daily Gratitude and Intention

Today I am grateful for:

........................................................................................................
........................................................................................................
........................................................................................................
........................................................................................................
........................................................................................................
........................................................................................................
........................................................................................................
........................................................................................................
........................................................................................................
........................................................................................................
........................................................................................................
........................................................................................................
........................................................................................................
........................................................................................................
........................................................................................................

Today's challenge and how it serves me to achieve my Life Priorities.

........................................................................................................
........................................................................................................
........................................................................................................
........................................................................................................
........................................................................................................

My highest Intentions for Tomorrow:

........................................................................................................
........................................................................................................
........................................................................................................
........................................................................................................
........................................................................................................

# JUN 13

*If you have true gratitude, it will express itself automatically. It will be visible in your eyes, around your being, in your aura. — Sri Chinmoy*

## Daily Gratitude and Intention

Today I am grateful for:

........................................................................................
........................................................................................
........................................................................................
........................................................................................
........................................................................................
........................................................................................
........................................................................................
........................................................................................
........................................................................................
........................................................................................
........................................................................................
........................................................................................
........................................................................................
........................................................................................
........................................................................................

Today's challenge and how it serves me to achieve my Life Priorities.

........................................................................................
........................................................................................
........................................................................................
........................................................................................
........................................................................................

My highest Intentions for Tomorrow:

........................................................................................
........................................................................................
........................................................................................
........................................................................................
........................................................................................

## Daily Gratitude and Intention

Today I am grateful for:

..............................................................................................................................
..............................................................................................................................
..............................................................................................................................
..............................................................................................................................
..............................................................................................................................
..............................................................................................................................
..............................................................................................................................
..............................................................................................................................
..............................................................................................................................
..............................................................................................................................
..............................................................................................................................
..............................................................................................................................

Today's challenge and how it serves me to achieve my Life Priorities.

..............................................................................................................................
..............................................................................................................................
..............................................................................................................................
..............................................................................................................................
..............................................................................................................................

My highest Intentions for Tomorrow:

..............................................................................................................................
..............................................................................................................................
..............................................................................................................................
..............................................................................................................................
..............................................................................................................................

# JUN 15

## Daily Gratitude and Intention

Today I am grateful for:

.............................................................................................

.............................................................................................

.............................................................................................

.............................................................................................

.............................................................................................

.............................................................................................

.............................................................................................

.............................................................................................

.............................................................................................

.............................................................................................

.............................................................................................

.............................................................................................

.............................................................................................

Today's challenge and how it serves me to achieve my Life Priorities.

.............................................................................................

.............................................................................................

.............................................................................................

.............................................................................................

.............................................................................................

My highest Intentions for Tomorrow:

.............................................................................................

.............................................................................................

.............................................................................................

.............................................................................................

.............................................................................................

*In a world where thrushes sing and willow trees are golden in the spring, boredom should have been included among the seven deadly sins. — Elizabeth Goudge*

# JUN 16

## Daily Gratitude and Intention

Today I am grateful for:

..................................................................................................
..................................................................................................
..................................................................................................
..................................................................................................
..................................................................................................
..................................................................................................
..................................................................................................
..................................................................................................
..................................................................................................
..................................................................................................
..................................................................................................
..................................................................................................

Today's challenge and how it serves me to achieve my Life Priorities.

..................................................................................................
..................................................................................................
..................................................................................................
..................................................................................................
..................................................................................................

My highest Intentions for Tomorrow:

..................................................................................................
..................................................................................................
..................................................................................................
..................................................................................................
..................................................................................................

# JUN 17

## Daily Gratitude and Intention

Today I am grateful for:

.................................................................................................
.................................................................................................
.................................................................................................
.................................................................................................
.................................................................................................
.................................................................................................
.................................................................................................
.................................................................................................
.................................................................................................
.................................................................................................
.................................................................................................
.................................................................................................
.................................................................................................

Today's challenge and how it serves me to achieve my Life Priorities.

.................................................................................................
.................................................................................................
.................................................................................................
.................................................................................................
.................................................................................................

My highest Intentions for Tomorrow:

.................................................................................................
.................................................................................................
.................................................................................................
.................................................................................................
.................................................................................................

*In daily life we must see that it is not happiness that makes us grateful, but gratefulness that makes us happy.*
*— Brother David Steindl-Rast*

JUN 18

## Daily Gratitude and Intention

Today I am grateful for:

..................................................................................................................
..................................................................................................................
..................................................................................................................
..................................................................................................................
..................................................................................................................
..................................................................................................................
..................................................................................................................
..................................................................................................................
..................................................................................................................
..................................................................................................................
..................................................................................................................
..................................................................................................................

Today's challenge and how it serves me to achieve my Life Priorities.

..................................................................................................................
..................................................................................................................
..................................................................................................................
..................................................................................................................
..................................................................................................................

My highest Intentions for Tomorrow:

..................................................................................................................
..................................................................................................................
..................................................................................................................
..................................................................................................................

# JUN 19

## Daily Gratitude and Intention

Today I am grateful for:

......................................................................................
......................................................................................
......................................................................................
......................................................................................
......................................................................................
......................................................................................
......................................................................................
......................................................................................
......................................................................................
......................................................................................
......................................................................................
......................................................................................
......................................................................................
......................................................................................

Today's challenge and how it serves me to achieve my Life Priorities.

......................................................................................
......................................................................................
......................................................................................
......................................................................................
......................................................................................

My highest Intentions for Tomorrow:

......................................................................................
......................................................................................
......................................................................................
......................................................................................
......................................................................................

*In life one has a choice to take one of two paths: to wait for some special day—or to celebrate each special day.*
*— Rasheed Ogunlaru*

JUN 20

## Daily Gratitude and Intention

Today I am grateful for:

.................................................................................................................................
.................................................................................................................................
.................................................................................................................................
.................................................................................................................................
.................................................................................................................................
.................................................................................................................................
.................................................................................................................................
.................................................................................................................................
.................................................................................................................................
.................................................................................................................................
.................................................................................................................................
.................................................................................................................................

Today's challenge and how it serves me to achieve my Life Priorities.

.................................................................................................................................
.................................................................................................................................
.................................................................................................................................
.................................................................................................................................
.................................................................................................................................

My highest Intentions for Tomorrow:

.................................................................................................................................
.................................................................................................................................
.................................................................................................................................
.................................................................................................................................
.................................................................................................................................

# JUN 21

## Daily Gratitude and Intention

Today I am grateful for:

........................................................................................................
........................................................................................................
........................................................................................................
........................................................................................................
........................................................................................................
........................................................................................................
........................................................................................................
........................................................................................................
........................................................................................................
........................................................................................................
........................................................................................................
........................................................................................................

Today's challenge and how it serves me to achieve my Life Priorities.

........................................................................................................
........................................................................................................
........................................................................................................
........................................................................................................
........................................................................................................

My highest Intentions for Tomorrow:

........................................................................................................
........................................................................................................
........................................................................................................
........................................................................................................
........................................................................................................

*In ordinary life we hardly realize that we receive a great deal more than we give, and that it is only with gratitude that life becomes rich.*
*— Dietrich Bonhoeffer*

## Daily Gratitude and Intention

Today I am grateful for:

..................................................................................................
..................................................................................................
..................................................................................................
..................................................................................................
..................................................................................................
..................................................................................................
..................................................................................................
..................................................................................................
..................................................................................................
..................................................................................................
..................................................................................................
..................................................................................................
..................................................................................................

Today's challenge and how it serves me to achieve my Life Priorities.

..................................................................................................
..................................................................................................
..................................................................................................
..................................................................................................
..................................................................................................
..................................................................................................

My highest Intentions for Tomorrow:

..................................................................................................
..................................................................................................
..................................................................................................
..................................................................................................
..................................................................................................

# JUN 23

## Daily Gratitude and Intention

Today I am grateful for:

..................................................................................................
..................................................................................................
..................................................................................................
..................................................................................................
..................................................................................................
..................................................................................................
..................................................................................................
..................................................................................................
..................................................................................................
..................................................................................................
..................................................................................................
..................................................................................................
..................................................................................................
..................................................................................................

Today's challenge and how it serves me to achieve my Life Priorities.

..................................................................................................
..................................................................................................
..................................................................................................
..................................................................................................
..................................................................................................
..................................................................................................

My highest Intentions for Tomorrow:

..................................................................................................
..................................................................................................
..................................................................................................
..................................................................................................
..................................................................................................

## Daily Gratitude and Intention

Today I am grateful for:

......................................................................................................
......................................................................................................
......................................................................................................
......................................................................................................
......................................................................................................
......................................................................................................
......................................................................................................
......................................................................................................
......................................................................................................
......................................................................................................
......................................................................................................
......................................................................................................
......................................................................................................
......................................................................................................

Today's challenge and how it serves me to achieve my Life Priorities.

......................................................................................................
......................................................................................................
......................................................................................................
......................................................................................................
......................................................................................................

My highest Intentions for Tomorrow:

......................................................................................................
......................................................................................................
......................................................................................................
......................................................................................................
......................................................................................................

# JUN 25

## Daily Gratitude and Intention

Today I am grateful for:

..................................................................................................
..................................................................................................
..................................................................................................
..................................................................................................
..................................................................................................
..................................................................................................
..................................................................................................
..................................................................................................
..................................................................................................
..................................................................................................
..................................................................................................
..................................................................................................
..................................................................................................
..................................................................................................
..................................................................................................

Today's challenge and how it serves me to achieve my Life Priorities.

..................................................................................................
..................................................................................................
..................................................................................................
..................................................................................................
..................................................................................................

My highest Intentions for Tomorrow:

..................................................................................................
..................................................................................................
..................................................................................................
..................................................................................................
..................................................................................................

*It's a sign of mediocrity when you demonstrate gratitude with moderation. — Roberto Benigni*

## Daily Gratitude and Intention

Today I am grateful for:

...............................................................................................................

...............................................................................................................

...............................................................................................................

...............................................................................................................

...............................................................................................................

...............................................................................................................

...............................................................................................................

...............................................................................................................

...............................................................................................................

...............................................................................................................

...............................................................................................................

...............................................................................................................

Today's challenge and how it serves me to achieve my Life Priorities.

...............................................................................................................

...............................................................................................................

...............................................................................................................

...............................................................................................................

...............................................................................................................

My highest Intentions for Tomorrow:

...............................................................................................................

...............................................................................................................

...............................................................................................................

...............................................................................................................

...............................................................................................................

# JUN 27

## Daily Gratitude and Intention

Today I am grateful for:

........................................................................................................
........................................................................................................
........................................................................................................
........................................................................................................
........................................................................................................
........................................................................................................
........................................................................................................
........................................................................................................
........................................................................................................
........................................................................................................
........................................................................................................
........................................................................................................
........................................................................................................

Today's challenge and how it serves me to achieve my Life Priorities.

........................................................................................................
........................................................................................................
........................................................................................................
........................................................................................................
........................................................................................................

My highest Intentions for Tomorrow:

........................................................................................................
........................................................................................................
........................................................................................................
........................................................................................................
........................................................................................................

*Joy is a heart full and a mind purified by gratitude.*
*— Marietta McCarty*

## Daily Gratitude and Intention

Today I am grateful for:

..................................................................................................
..................................................................................................
..................................................................................................
..................................................................................................
..................................................................................................
..................................................................................................
..................................................................................................
..................................................................................................
..................................................................................................
..................................................................................................
..................................................................................................
..................................................................................................

Today's challenge and how it serves me to achieve my Life Priorities.

..................................................................................................
..................................................................................................
..................................................................................................
..................................................................................................
..................................................................................................

My highest Intentions for Tomorrow:

..................................................................................................
..................................................................................................
..................................................................................................
..................................................................................................
..................................................................................................

# JUN 29

*Joy is the simplest form of gratitude. — Karth Barth*

## Daily Gratitude and Intention

Today I am grateful for:

.................................................................................................................
.................................................................................................................
.................................................................................................................
.................................................................................................................
.................................................................................................................
.................................................................................................................
.................................................................................................................
.................................................................................................................
.................................................................................................................
.................................................................................................................
.................................................................................................................
.................................................................................................................
.................................................................................................................
.................................................................................................................

Today's challenge and how it serves me to achieve my Life Priorities.

.................................................................................................................
.................................................................................................................
.................................................................................................................
.................................................................................................................
.................................................................................................................
.................................................................................................................

My highest Intentions for Tomorrow:

.................................................................................................................
.................................................................................................................
.................................................................................................................
.................................................................................................................
.................................................................................................................

*Just an observation: it is impossible to be both grateful and depressed. Those with a grateful mindset tend to see the message in the mess. And even though life may knock them down, the grateful find reasons, if even small ones, to get up.* — Steve Maraboli

## Daily Gratitude and Intention

Today I am grateful for:

.................................................................................................................

.................................................................................................................

.................................................................................................................

.................................................................................................................

.................................................................................................................

.................................................................................................................

.................................................................................................................

.................................................................................................................

.................................................................................................................

.................................................................................................................

.................................................................................................................

.................................................................................................................

Today's challenge and how it serves me to achieve my Life Priorities.

.................................................................................................................

.................................................................................................................

.................................................................................................................

.................................................................................................................

.................................................................................................................

My highest Intentions for Tomorrow:

.................................................................................................................

.................................................................................................................

.................................................................................................................

.................................................................................................................

# JULY

## Monthly Intention Plan

Write the top priorities you intend to focus on in each area of your life during this month.

SPIRITUAL

..................................................................................................................
..................................................................................................................
..................................................................................................................
..................................................................................................................
..................................................................................................................
..................................................................................................................
..................................................................................................................

MENTAL / EDUCATION

..................................................................................................................
..................................................................................................................
..................................................................................................................
..................................................................................................................
..................................................................................................................
..................................................................................................................
..................................................................................................................

VOCATIONAL / CAREER

..................................................................................................................
..................................................................................................................
..................................................................................................................
..................................................................................................................
..................................................................................................................
..................................................................................................................
..................................................................................................................

## FINANCIAL / SAVING & INVESTING

......................................................................................................
......................................................................................................
......................................................................................................
......................................................................................................
......................................................................................................
......................................................................................................
......................................................................................................

## FAMILIAL / RELATIONSHIP

......................................................................................................
......................................................................................................
......................................................................................................
......................................................................................................
......................................................................................................
......................................................................................................
......................................................................................................
......................................................................................................

## SOCIAL / FRIENDS

......................................................................................................
......................................................................................................
......................................................................................................
......................................................................................................
......................................................................................................
......................................................................................................
......................................................................................................
......................................................................................................

## HEALTH & PHYSICAL APPEARANCE

......................................................................................................
......................................................................................................
......................................................................................................
......................................................................................................
......................................................................................................
......................................................................................................
......................................................................................................

# JUL 1

*Just as millions of snowflakes pile up to create a blanket of snow, the thank you's we say pile up and fall gently upon one another until, in our hearts and minds, we are adrift in gratitude.*
*— Daphne Rose Kingman*

## Daily Gratitude and Intention

Today I am grateful for:

.......................................................................................................

.......................................................................................................

.......................................................................................................

.......................................................................................................

.......................................................................................................

.......................................................................................................

.......................................................................................................

.......................................................................................................

.......................................................................................................

.......................................................................................................

.......................................................................................................

.......................................................................................................

Today's challenge and how it serves me to achieve my Life Priorities.

.......................................................................................................

.......................................................................................................

.......................................................................................................

.......................................................................................................

.......................................................................................................

My highest Intentions for Tomorrow:

.......................................................................................................

.......................................................................................................

.......................................................................................................

.......................................................................................................

.......................................................................................................

*Kindness trumps greed: it asks for sharing. Kindness trumps fear: it calls forth gratefulness and love. Kindness trumps even stupidity, for with sharing and love, one learns. — Marc Estrin*

JUL 2

## Daily Gratitude and Intention

Today I am grateful for:

..................................................................................................................................
..................................................................................................................................
..................................................................................................................................
..................................................................................................................................
..................................................................................................................................
..................................................................................................................................
..................................................................................................................................
..................................................................................................................................
..................................................................................................................................
..................................................................................................................................
..................................................................................................................................

Today's challenge and how it serves me to achieve my Life Priorities.

..................................................................................................................................
..................................................................................................................................
..................................................................................................................................
..................................................................................................................................

My highest Intentions for Tomorrow:

..................................................................................................................................
..................................................................................................................................
..................................................................................................................................
..................................................................................................................................

# JUL 3

## Daily Gratitude and Intention

Today I am grateful for:

........................................................................................

........................................................................................

........................................................................................

........................................................................................

........................................................................................

........................................................................................

........................................................................................

........................................................................................

........................................................................................

........................................................................................

........................................................................................

........................................................................................

........................................................................................

Today's challenge and how it serves me to achieve my Life Priorities.

........................................................................................

........................................................................................

........................................................................................

........................................................................................

........................................................................................

My highest Intentions for Tomorrow:

........................................................................................

........................................................................................

........................................................................................

........................................................................................

........................................................................................

Let gratitude be the pillow upon which you kneel to say your nightly prayer. And let faith be the bridge you build to overcome evil and welcome good. — Maya Angelou

## Daily Gratitude and Intention

Today I am grateful for:

........................................................................................................................

........................................................................................................................

........................................................................................................................

........................................................................................................................

........................................................................................................................

........................................................................................................................

........................................................................................................................

........................................................................................................................

........................................................................................................................

........................................................................................................................

........................................................................................................................

........................................................................................................................

Today's challenge and how it serves me to achieve my Life Priorities.

........................................................................................................................

........................................................................................................................

........................................................................................................................

........................................................................................................................

........................................................................................................................

My highest Intentions for Tomorrow:

........................................................................................................................

........................................................................................................................

........................................................................................................................

........................................................................................................................

........................................................................................................................

# JUL 5

## Daily Gratitude and Intention

Today I am grateful for:

........................................................................................................
........................................................................................................
........................................................................................................
........................................................................................................
........................................................................................................
........................................................................................................
........................................................................................................
........................................................................................................
........................................................................................................
........................................................................................................
........................................................................................................
........................................................................................................
........................................................................................................

Today's challenge and how it serves me to achieve my Life Priorities.

........................................................................................................
........................................................................................................
........................................................................................................
........................................................................................................
........................................................................................................
........................................................................................................

My highest Intentions for Tomorrow:

........................................................................................................
........................................................................................................
........................................................................................................
........................................................................................................
........................................................................................................

*Let us remember that, as much has been given us, much will be expected from us, and that true homage comes from the heart as well as from the lips, and shows itself in deeds.*
— *Theodore Roosevelt*

## Daily Gratitude and Intention

Today I am grateful for:

........................................................................................................

........................................................................................................

........................................................................................................

........................................................................................................

........................................................................................................

........................................................................................................

........................................................................................................

........................................................................................................

........................................................................................................

........................................................................................................

........................................................................................................

........................................................................................................

Today's challenge and how it serves me to achieve my Life Priorities.

........................................................................................................

........................................................................................................

........................................................................................................

........................................................................................................

........................................................................................................

My highest Intentions for Tomorrow:

........................................................................................................

........................................................................................................

........................................................................................................

........................................................................................................

........................................................................................................

# JUL 7

*Let us rise up and be thankful, for if we didn't learn a lot today, at least we learned a little, and if we didn't learn a little, at least we didn't get sick, and if we got sick, at least we didn't die; so, let us all be thankful. — Buddha*

## Daily Gratitude and Intention

Today I am grateful for:

.............................................................................................
.............................................................................................
.............................................................................................
.............................................................................................
.............................................................................................
.............................................................................................
.............................................................................................
.............................................................................................
.............................................................................................
.............................................................................................
.............................................................................................
.............................................................................................
.............................................................................................
.............................................................................................

Today's challenge and how it serves me to achieve my Life Priorities.

.............................................................................................
.............................................................................................
.............................................................................................
.............................................................................................
.............................................................................................
.............................................................................................

My highest Intentions for Tomorrow:

.............................................................................................
.............................................................................................
.............................................................................................
.............................................................................................
.............................................................................................

*Life-changing gratitude does not fasten to a life unless nailed through with one very specific nail at a time. — Ann Voskamp*

# JUL 8

## Daily Gratitude and Intention

Today I am grateful for:

.........................................................................................................
.........................................................................................................
.........................................................................................................
.........................................................................................................
.........................................................................................................
.........................................................................................................
.........................................................................................................
.........................................................................................................
.........................................................................................................
.........................................................................................................
.........................................................................................................
.........................................................................................................
.........................................................................................................

Today's challenge and how it serves me to achieve my Life Priorities.

.........................................................................................................
.........................................................................................................
.........................................................................................................
.........................................................................................................
.........................................................................................................

My highest Intentions for Tomorrow:

.........................................................................................................
.........................................................................................................
.........................................................................................................
.........................................................................................................
.........................................................................................................

# JUL 9

## Daily Gratitude and Intention

Today I am grateful for:

.............................................................................
.............................................................................
.............................................................................
.............................................................................
.............................................................................
.............................................................................
.............................................................................
.............................................................................
.............................................................................
.............................................................................
.............................................................................
.............................................................................
.............................................................................

Today's challenge and how it serves me to achieve my Life Priorities.

.............................................................................
.............................................................................
.............................................................................
.............................................................................
.............................................................................

My highest Intentions for Tomorrow:

.............................................................................
.............................................................................
.............................................................................
.............................................................................
.............................................................................

*Love of God is pure when joy and suffering inspire an equal degree of gratitude. — Simone Weil*

## Daily Gratitude and Intention

Today I am grateful for:

.......................................................................................................................................
.......................................................................................................................................
.......................................................................................................................................
.......................................................................................................................................
.......................................................................................................................................
.......................................................................................................................................
.......................................................................................................................................
.......................................................................................................................................
.......................................................................................................................................
.......................................................................................................................................
.......................................................................................................................................
.......................................................................................................................................

Today's challenge and how it serves me to achieve my Life Priorities.

.......................................................................................................................................
.......................................................................................................................................
.......................................................................................................................................
.......................................................................................................................................

My highest Intentions for Tomorrow:

.......................................................................................................................................
.......................................................................................................................................
.......................................................................................................................................
.......................................................................................................................................

# JUL 11

## Daily Gratitude and Intention

Today I am grateful for:

....................................................................................................
....................................................................................................
....................................................................................................
....................................................................................................
....................................................................................................
....................................................................................................
....................................................................................................
....................................................................................................
....................................................................................................
....................................................................................................
....................................................................................................
....................................................................................................
....................................................................................................

Today's challenge and how it serves me to achieve my Life Priorities.

....................................................................................................
....................................................................................................
....................................................................................................
....................................................................................................
....................................................................................................

My highest Intentions for Tomorrow:

....................................................................................................
....................................................................................................
....................................................................................................
....................................................................................................
....................................................................................................

*Make a pact with yourself today to not be defined by your past. Sometimes the greatest thing to come out of all your hard work isn't what you get for it, but what you become for it. Shake things up today! Be You... Be Free... Share.*
— Steve Maraboli

## Daily Gratitude and Intention

Today I am grateful for:

..................................................................................................................
..................................................................................................................
..................................................................................................................
..................................................................................................................
..................................................................................................................
..................................................................................................................
..................................................................................................................
..................................................................................................................
..................................................................................................................
..................................................................................................................
..................................................................................................................
..................................................................................................................

Today's challenge and how it serves me to achieve my Life Priorities.

..................................................................................................................
..................................................................................................................
..................................................................................................................
..................................................................................................................
..................................................................................................................

My highest Intentions for Tomorrow:

..................................................................................................................
..................................................................................................................
..................................................................................................................
..................................................................................................................
..................................................................................................................

# JUL 13

*Make a point to say thank you to someone today.*
*— Deborah Norville*

## Daily Gratitude and Intention

Today I am grateful for:

..............................................................................................................
..............................................................................................................
..............................................................................................................
..............................................................................................................
..............................................................................................................
..............................................................................................................
..............................................................................................................
..............................................................................................................
..............................................................................................................
..............................................................................................................
..............................................................................................................
..............................................................................................................
..............................................................................................................

Today's challenge and how it serves me to achieve my Life Priorities.

..............................................................................................................
..............................................................................................................
..............................................................................................................
..............................................................................................................
..............................................................................................................

My highest Intentions for Tomorrow:

..............................................................................................................
..............................................................................................................
..............................................................................................................
..............................................................................................................
..............................................................................................................

*Make it a habit to tell people thank you. To express your appreciation, sincerely and without the expectation of anything in return. Truly appreciate those around you, and you'll soon find many others around you. Truly appreciate life, and you'll find that you have more of it. — Ralph Marston*

## Daily Gratitude and Intention

Today I am grateful for:

..................................................................................................................................
..................................................................................................................................
..................................................................................................................................
..................................................................................................................................
..................................................................................................................................
..................................................................................................................................
..................................................................................................................................
..................................................................................................................................
..................................................................................................................................
..................................................................................................................................
..................................................................................................................................
..................................................................................................................................

Today's challenge and how it serves me to achieve my Life Priorities.

..................................................................................................................................
..................................................................................................................................
..................................................................................................................................
..................................................................................................................................
..................................................................................................................................

My highest Intentions for Tomorrow:

..................................................................................................................................
..................................................................................................................................
..................................................................................................................................
..................................................................................................................................
..................................................................................................................................

# JUL 15

*Many people who order their lives rightly in all other ways are kept in poverty by their lack of gratitude.*
*— Wallace Wattles*

## Daily Gratitude and Intention

Today I am grateful for:

..................................................................................................................

..................................................................................................................

..................................................................................................................

..................................................................................................................

..................................................................................................................

..................................................................................................................

..................................................................................................................

..................................................................................................................

..................................................................................................................

..................................................................................................................

..................................................................................................................

..................................................................................................................

Today's challenge and how it serves me to achieve my Life Priorities.

..................................................................................................................

..................................................................................................................

..................................................................................................................

..................................................................................................................

..................................................................................................................

My highest Intentions for Tomorrow:

..................................................................................................................

..................................................................................................................

..................................................................................................................

..................................................................................................................

*May your days be filled with Abundance, Joy and Gratitude to God, for all the gifts you have received and have yet to receive! — Lisa Ladrido*

## Daily Gratitude and Intention

Today I am grateful for:

..............................................................................................................................
..............................................................................................................................
..............................................................................................................................
..............................................................................................................................
..............................................................................................................................
..............................................................................................................................
..............................................................................................................................
..............................................................................................................................
..............................................................................................................................
..............................................................................................................................
..............................................................................................................................
..............................................................................................................................

Today's challenge and how it serves me to achieve my Life Priorities.

..............................................................................................................................
..............................................................................................................................
..............................................................................................................................
..............................................................................................................................
..............................................................................................................................

My highest Intentions for Tomorrow:

..............................................................................................................................
..............................................................................................................................
..............................................................................................................................
..............................................................................................................................
..............................................................................................................................

# JUL 17

## Daily Gratitude and Intention

Today I am grateful for:

.............................................................................................................................
.............................................................................................................................
.............................................................................................................................
.............................................................................................................................
.............................................................................................................................
.............................................................................................................................
.............................................................................................................................
.............................................................................................................................
.............................................................................................................................
.............................................................................................................................
.............................................................................................................................
.............................................................................................................................

Today's challenge and how it serves me to achieve my Life Priorities.

.............................................................................................................................
.............................................................................................................................
.............................................................................................................................
.............................................................................................................................
.............................................................................................................................

My highest Intentions for Tomorrow:

.............................................................................................................................
.............................................................................................................................
.............................................................................................................................
.............................................................................................................................
.............................................................................................................................

*Most of us forget to take time for wonder, praise and gratitude until it is almost too late. Gratitude is a many-colored quality, reaching in all directions. It goes out for small things and for large; it is a God-ward going. — Faith Baldwin*

## Daily Gratitude and Intention

Today I am grateful for:

...................................................................................................
...................................................................................................
...................................................................................................
...................................................................................................
...................................................................................................
...................................................................................................
...................................................................................................
...................................................................................................
...................................................................................................
...................................................................................................
...................................................................................................
...................................................................................................

Today's challenge and how it serves me to achieve my Life Priorities.

...................................................................................................
...................................................................................................
...................................................................................................
...................................................................................................
...................................................................................................

My highest Intentions for Tomorrow:

...................................................................................................
...................................................................................................
...................................................................................................
...................................................................................................
...................................................................................................

# JUL 19

## Daily Gratitude and Intention

Today I am grateful for:

...........................................................................................................................
...........................................................................................................................
...........................................................................................................................
...........................................................................................................................
...........................................................................................................................
...........................................................................................................................
...........................................................................................................................
...........................................................................................................................
...........................................................................................................................
...........................................................................................................................
...........................................................................................................................
...........................................................................................................................

Today's challenge and how it serves me to achieve my Life Priorities.

...........................................................................................................................
...........................................................................................................................
...........................................................................................................................
...........................................................................................................................
...........................................................................................................................

My highest Intentions for Tomorrow:

...........................................................................................................................
...........................................................................................................................
...........................................................................................................................
...........................................................................................................................
...........................................................................................................................

*My heart's gratitude is my life's plenitude.*
*— Sri Chinmoy*

## Daily Gratitude and Intention

Today I am grateful for:

........................................................................................

........................................................................................

........................................................................................

........................................................................................

........................................................................................

........................................................................................

........................................................................................

........................................................................................

........................................................................................

........................................................................................

........................................................................................

........................................................................................

........................................................................................

........................................................................................

Today's challenge and how it serves me to achieve my Life Priorities.

........................................................................................

........................................................................................

........................................................................................

........................................................................................

........................................................................................

........................................................................................

My highest Intentions for Tomorrow:

........................................................................................

........................................................................................

........................................................................................

........................................................................................

........................................................................................

........................................................................................

OptimumThinking.net

# JUL 21

*To be conscious of gratitude is to acknowledge a gift.*
*— Josef Pieper*

## Daily Gratitude and Intention

Today I am grateful for:

.......................................................................................................................................
.......................................................................................................................................
.......................................................................................................................................
.......................................................................................................................................
.......................................................................................................................................
.......................................................................................................................................
.......................................................................................................................................
.......................................................................................................................................
.......................................................................................................................................
.......................................................................................................................................
.......................................................................................................................................
.......................................................................................................................................
.......................................................................................................................................
.......................................................................................................................................

Today's challenge and how it serves me to achieve my Life Priorities.

.......................................................................................................................................
.......................................................................................................................................
.......................................................................................................................................
.......................................................................................................................................
.......................................................................................................................................
.......................................................................................................................................

My highest Intentions for Tomorrow:

.......................................................................................................................................
.......................................................................................................................................
.......................................................................................................................................
.......................................................................................................................................
.......................................................................................................................................

No one who achieves success does so without acknowledging the help of others. The wise and confident acknowledge this help with gratitude.
— Alfred North Whitehead

## Daily Gratitude and Intention

Today I am grateful for:

Today's challenge and how it serves me to achieve my Life Priorities.

made me
/ feel upset +
uncomfortable -

SL - slagged off our business — to me /
me business
at dinner / restaurant

↓ Benefit / service to me in me moment:
1/ made me deal with awkward situ.;
2/ practising skill of listening to criticism;
3/ because they raised it - OTS put me
other side across - so i heard someone
else's perception;
4/ understanding there are negative
perceptions of our business and it
can't be all rosy all of the time.
5/ made me learn to speak up against
them. / not so afraid of
disagreeing with me.

My highest Intentions for Tomorrow:

# JUL 23

## Daily Gratitude and Intention

Today I am grateful for:

.......................................................................................................................................................
.......................................................................................................................................................
.......................................................................................................................................................
.......................................................................................................................................................
.......................................................................................................................................................
.......................................................................................................................................................
.......................................................................................................................................................
.......................................................................................................................................................
.......................................................................................................................................................
.......................................................................................................................................................
.......................................................................................................................................................
.......................................................................................................................................................

Today's challenge and how it serves me to achieve my Life Priorities.

.......................................................................................................................................................
.......................................................................................................................................................
.......................................................................................................................................................
.......................................................................................................................................................
.......................................................................................................................................................

My highest Intentions for Tomorrow:

.......................................................................................................................................................
.......................................................................................................................................................
.......................................................................................................................................................
.......................................................................................................................................................
.......................................................................................................................................................

*Now there are many, many people in the world, but relatively few with whom we interact, and even fewer who cause us problems. So, when you come across such a chance for practicing patience and tolerance, you should treat it with gratitude. It is rare. — Dalai Lama*

# JUL 24

## Daily Gratitude and Intention

Today I am grateful for:

..................................................................................................
..................................................................................................
..................................................................................................
..................................................................................................
..................................................................................................
..................................................................................................
..................................................................................................
..................................................................................................
..................................................................................................
..................................................................................................
..................................................................................................

Today's challenge and how it serves me to achieve my Life Priorities.

..................................................................................................
..................................................................................................
..................................................................................................
..................................................................................................
..................................................................................................

My highest Intentions for Tomorrow:

..................................................................................................
..................................................................................................
..................................................................................................
..................................................................................................
..................................................................................................

# JUL 25

*O Lord that lends me life, Lend me a heart replete with thankfulness! — William Shakespeare*

## Daily Gratitude and Intention

Today I am grateful for:

........................................................................

........................................................................

........................................................................

........................................................................

........................................................................

........................................................................

........................................................................

........................................................................

........................................................................

........................................................................

........................................................................

........................................................................

........................................................................

Today's challenge and how it serves me to achieve my Life Priorities.

........................................................................

........................................................................

........................................................................

........................................................................

........................................................................

My highest Intentions for Tomorrow:

........................................................................

........................................................................

........................................................................

........................................................................

One looks back with appreciation to the brilliant teachers, but with gratitude to those who touched our human feelings. The curriculum is so much necessary raw material, but warmth is the vital element for the growing plant and for the soul of the child. — Carl Jung

# JUL 26

## Daily Gratitude and Intention

Today I am grateful for:

........................................................................................................

........................................................................................................

........................................................................................................

........................................................................................................

........................................................................................................

........................................................................................................

........................................................................................................

........................................................................................................

........................................................................................................

........................................................................................................

........................................................................................................

........................................................................................................

Today's challenge and how it serves me to achieve my Life Priorities.

........................................................................................................

........................................................................................................

........................................................................................................

........................................................................................................

My highest Intentions for Tomorrow:

........................................................................................................

........................................................................................................

........................................................................................................

........................................................................................................

# JUL 27

One of the surest evidences of friendship that one individual can display to another is telling him gently of a fault. If any other can excel it, it is listening to such a disclosure with gratitude, and amending the error.
— Edward G. Bulwer-Lytton

## Daily Gratitude and Intention

Today I am grateful for:

..................................................................................................................
..................................................................................................................
..................................................................................................................
..................................................................................................................
..................................................................................................................
..................................................................................................................
..................................................................................................................
..................................................................................................................
..................................................................................................................
..................................................................................................................
..................................................................................................................
..................................................................................................................
..................................................................................................................

Today's challenge and how it serves me to achieve my Life Priorities.

..................................................................................................................
..................................................................................................................
..................................................................................................................
..................................................................................................................
..................................................................................................................

My highest Intentions for Tomorrow:

..................................................................................................................
..................................................................................................................
..................................................................................................................
..................................................................................................................
..................................................................................................................

One regret dear world, that I am determined not to
have when I am lying on my deathbed is that I did
not kiss you enough. — Hafiz of Persia

JUL 28

## Daily Gratitude and Intention

Today I am grateful for:

........................................................................................................

........................................................................................................

........................................................................................................

........................................................................................................

........................................................................................................

........................................................................................................

........................................................................................................

........................................................................................................

........................................................................................................

........................................................................................................

........................................................................................................

Today's challenge and how it serves me to achieve my Life Priorities.

........................................................................................................

........................................................................................................

........................................................................................................

........................................................................................................

My highest Intentions for Tomorrow:

........................................................................................................

........................................................................................................

........................................................................................................

........................................................................................................

........................................................................................................

*Only a stomach that rarely feels hungry scorns common things. — Horace*

## Daily Gratitude and Intention

Today I am grateful for:

1. Abundance of financial means - so i can send Ava to a lovely school + tennis camp.

2. A lovely team at work. Interesting work to do.

3. A beautiful home + family

4. An evening with Ava uninterrupted by work.

Today's challenge and how it serves me to achieve my Life Priorities.

Eating well + not binging on sugar. Constant challenge to make better food choices. I have to keep trying. If i get it, make better choices i will live longer; show Ava how to eat better; have more energy; feel less bloated; more positive; more sexy

My highest Intentions for Tomorrow:

Make good/healthy food choices. Avoid high sugar foods. Avoid sugary drinks. Be productive / Be calm. Breathe through any craving - try it just for today.

*Paying tax should be framed as a glorious civic duty worthy of gratitude—not a punishment for making money. — Alain de Botton*

# JUL 30

## Daily Gratitude and Intention

Today I am grateful for:

......................................................................................................
......................................................................................................
......................................................................................................
......................................................................................................
......................................................................................................
......................................................................................................
......................................................................................................
......................................................................................................
......................................................................................................
......................................................................................................
......................................................................................................
......................................................................................................

Today's challenge and how it serves me to achieve my Life Priorities.

......................................................................................................
......................................................................................................
......................................................................................................
......................................................................................................
......................................................................................................

My highest Intentions for Tomorrow:

......................................................................................................
......................................................................................................
......................................................................................................
......................................................................................................
......................................................................................................

# JUL 31

*Piglet noticed that even though he had a Very Small Heart, it could hold a rather large amount of Gratitude.*
*— A.A. Milne*

## Daily Gratitude and Intention

Today I am grateful for:

.......................................................................................................
.......................................................................................................
.......................................................................................................
.......................................................................................................
.......................................................................................................
.......................................................................................................
.......................................................................................................
.......................................................................................................
.......................................................................................................
.......................................................................................................
.......................................................................................................
.......................................................................................................

Today's challenge and how it serves me to achieve my Life Priorities.

.......................................................................................................
.......................................................................................................
.......................................................................................................
.......................................................................................................
.......................................................................................................

My highest Intentions for Tomorrow:

.......................................................................................................
.......................................................................................................
.......................................................................................................
.......................................................................................................
.......................................................................................................

Life flows freely when we
express our gratitude daily.

# AUGUST

## Monthly Intention Plan

Write the top priorities you intend to focus on in each area of your life during this month.

SPIRITUAL

.....................................................................................................................................
.....................................................................................................................................
.....................................................................................................................................
.....................................................................................................................................
.....................................................................................................................................
.....................................................................................................................................
.....................................................................................................................................

MENTAL / EDUCATION

.....................................................................................................................................
.....................................................................................................................................
.....................................................................................................................................
.....................................................................................................................................
.....................................................................................................................................
.....................................................................................................................................
.....................................................................................................................................
.....................................................................................................................................

VOCATIONAL / CAREER

.....................................................................................................................................
.....................................................................................................................................
.....................................................................................................................................
.....................................................................................................................................
.....................................................................................................................................
.....................................................................................................................................
.....................................................................................................................................
.....................................................................................................................................

## FINANCIAL / SAVING & INVESTING

..............................................................................................................
..............................................................................................................
..............................................................................................................
..............................................................................................................
..............................................................................................................
..............................................................................................................
..............................................................................................................

## FAMILIAL / RELATIONSHIP

..............................................................................................................
..............................................................................................................
..............................................................................................................
..............................................................................................................
..............................................................................................................
..............................................................................................................
..............................................................................................................

## SOCIAL / FRIENDS

..............................................................................................................
..............................................................................................................
..............................................................................................................
..............................................................................................................
..............................................................................................................
..............................................................................................................
..............................................................................................................

## HEALTH & PHYSICAL APPEARANCE

..............................................................................................................
..............................................................................................................
..............................................................................................................
..............................................................................................................
..............................................................................................................
..............................................................................................................
..............................................................................................................

# AUG 1

## Daily Gratitude and Intention

Today I am grateful for:

.........................................................................................................

.........................................................................................................

.........................................................................................................

.........................................................................................................

.........................................................................................................

.........................................................................................................

.........................................................................................................

.........................................................................................................

.........................................................................................................

.........................................................................................................

.........................................................................................................

.........................................................................................................

.........................................................................................................

Today's challenge and how it serves me to achieve my Life Priorities.

.........................................................................................................

.........................................................................................................

.........................................................................................................

.........................................................................................................

.........................................................................................................

.........................................................................................................

My highest Intentions for Tomorrow:

.........................................................................................................

.........................................................................................................

.........................................................................................................

.........................................................................................................

.........................................................................................................

## Daily Gratitude and Intention

Today I am grateful for:

......................................................................................................
......................................................................................................
......................................................................................................
......................................................................................................
......................................................................................................
......................................................................................................
......................................................................................................
......................................................................................................
......................................................................................................
......................................................................................................
......................................................................................................
......................................................................................................

Today's challenge and how it serves me to achieve my Life Priorities.

......................................................................................................
......................................................................................................
......................................................................................................
......................................................................................................
......................................................................................................

My highest Intentions for Tomorrow:

......................................................................................................
......................................................................................................
......................................................................................................
......................................................................................................
......................................................................................................

# AUG 3

## Daily Gratitude and Intention

Today I am grateful for:

........................................................................................................................

........................................................................................................................

........................................................................................................................

........................................................................................................................

........................................................................................................................

........................................................................................................................

........................................................................................................................

........................................................................................................................

........................................................................................................................

........................................................................................................................

........................................................................................................................

Today's challenge and how it serves me to achieve my Life Priorities.

........................................................................................................................

........................................................................................................................

........................................................................................................................

........................................................................................................................

........................................................................................................................

My highest Intentions for Tomorrow:

........................................................................................................................

........................................................................................................................

........................................................................................................................

........................................................................................................................

........................................................................................................................

*Reflect upon your present blessings, of which every man has plenty; not on your past misfortunes, of which all men have some.*
*— Charles Dickens*

# AUG 4

## Daily Gratitude and Intention

Today I am grateful for:

..............................................................................................................
..............................................................................................................
..............................................................................................................
..............................................................................................................
..............................................................................................................
..............................................................................................................
..............................................................................................................
..............................................................................................................
..............................................................................................................
..............................................................................................................
..............................................................................................................
..............................................................................................................

Today's challenge and how it serves me to achieve my Life Priorities.

..............................................................................................................
..............................................................................................................
..............................................................................................................
..............................................................................................................
..............................................................................................................

My highest Intentions for Tomorrow:

..............................................................................................................
..............................................................................................................
..............................................................................................................
..............................................................................................................
..............................................................................................................

# AUG 5

## Daily Gratitude and Intention

Today I am grateful for:

..................................................................................................
..................................................................................................
..................................................................................................
..................................................................................................
..................................................................................................
..................................................................................................
..................................................................................................
..................................................................................................
..................................................................................................
..................................................................................................
..................................................................................................
..................................................................................................

Today's challenge and how it serves me to achieve my Life Priorities.

..................................................................................................
..................................................................................................
..................................................................................................
..................................................................................................
..................................................................................................

My highest Intentions for Tomorrow:

..................................................................................................
..................................................................................................
..................................................................................................
..................................................................................................
..................................................................................................

## Daily Gratitude and Intention

Today I am grateful for:

......................................................................................................
......................................................................................................
......................................................................................................
......................................................................................................
......................................................................................................
......................................................................................................
......................................................................................................
......................................................................................................
......................................................................................................
......................................................................................................
......................................................................................................
......................................................................................................

Today's challenge and how it serves me to achieve my Life Priorities.

......................................................................................................
......................................................................................................
......................................................................................................
......................................................................................................
......................................................................................................

My highest Intentions for Tomorrow:

......................................................................................................
......................................................................................................
......................................................................................................
......................................................................................................

# AUG 7

## Daily Gratitude and Intention

Today I am grateful for:

.....................................................................................................
.....................................................................................................
.....................................................................................................
.....................................................................................................
.....................................................................................................
.....................................................................................................
.....................................................................................................
.....................................................................................................
.....................................................................................................
.....................................................................................................
.....................................................................................................
.....................................................................................................
.....................................................................................................
.....................................................................................................

Today's challenge and how it serves me to achieve my Life Priorities.

.....................................................................................................
.....................................................................................................
.....................................................................................................
.....................................................................................................
.....................................................................................................

My highest Intentions for Tomorrow:

.....................................................................................................
.....................................................................................................
.....................................................................................................
.....................................................................................................
.....................................................................................................

*Silent gratitude isn't much use to anyone. — G.B. Stern*

# Daily Gratitude and Intention

Today I am grateful for:

.................................................................................................

.................................................................................................

.................................................................................................

.................................................................................................

.................................................................................................

.................................................................................................

.................................................................................................

.................................................................................................

.................................................................................................

.................................................................................................

.................................................................................................

.................................................................................................

Today's challenge and how it serves me to achieve my Life Priorities.

.................................................................................................

.................................................................................................

.................................................................................................

.................................................................................................

My highest Intentions for Tomorrow:

.................................................................................................

.................................................................................................

.................................................................................................

.................................................................................................

.................................................................................................

# AUG 9

*So much about living life, to me, is about humility and gratitude. — Katherine Heigl*

## Daily Gratitude and Intention

Today I am grateful for:

........................................................................................

........................................................................................

........................................................................................

........................................................................................

........................................................................................

........................................................................................

........................................................................................

........................................................................................

........................................................................................

........................................................................................

........................................................................................

........................................................................................

........................................................................................

Today's challenge and how it serves me to achieve my Life Priorities.

........................................................................................

........................................................................................

........................................................................................

........................................................................................

........................................................................................

My highest Intentions for Tomorrow:

........................................................................................

........................................................................................

........................................................................................

........................................................................................

## Daily Gratitude and Intention

Today I am grateful for:

.................................................................................
.................................................................................
.................................................................................
.................................................................................
.................................................................................
.................................................................................
.................................................................................
.................................................................................
.................................................................................
.................................................................................
.................................................................................
.................................................................................
.................................................................................
.................................................................................

Today's challenge and how it serves me to achieve my Life Priorities.

.................................................................................
.................................................................................
.................................................................................
.................................................................................
.................................................................................

My highest Intentions for Tomorrow:

.................................................................................
.................................................................................
.................................................................................
.................................................................................
.................................................................................

# AUG 11

## Daily Gratitude and Intention

Today I am grateful for:

..................................................................................................
..................................................................................................
..................................................................................................
..................................................................................................
..................................................................................................
..................................................................................................
..................................................................................................
..................................................................................................
..................................................................................................
..................................................................................................
..................................................................................................

Today's challenge and how it serves me to achieve my Life Priorities.

..................................................................................................
..................................................................................................
..................................................................................................
..................................................................................................
..................................................................................................

My highest Intentions for Tomorrow:

..................................................................................................
..................................................................................................
..................................................................................................
..................................................................................................
..................................................................................................

*Take full account of what Excellencies which you possess, and in gratitude remember how you would hanker after them, if you had them not. — Marcus Aurelius*

# AUG 12

## Daily Gratitude and Intention

Today I am grateful for:

.................................................................................................
.................................................................................................
.................................................................................................
.................................................................................................
.................................................................................................
.................................................................................................
.................................................................................................
.................................................................................................
.................................................................................................
.................................................................................................
.................................................................................................
.................................................................................................
.................................................................................................

Today's challenge and how it serves me to achieve my Life Priorities.

.................................................................................................
.................................................................................................
.................................................................................................
.................................................................................................
.................................................................................................

My highest Intentions for Tomorrow:

.................................................................................................
.................................................................................................
.................................................................................................
.................................................................................................
.................................................................................................

**Optimum**Thinking.net

# AUG 13

## Daily Gratitude and Intention

Today I am grateful for:

.......................................................................................................................
.......................................................................................................................
.......................................................................................................................
.......................................................................................................................
.......................................................................................................................
.......................................................................................................................
.......................................................................................................................
.......................................................................................................................
.......................................................................................................................
.......................................................................................................................
.......................................................................................................................
.......................................................................................................................

Today's challenge and how it serves me to achieve my Life Priorities.

.......................................................................................................................
.......................................................................................................................
.......................................................................................................................
.......................................................................................................................
.......................................................................................................................

My highest Intentions for Tomorrow:

.......................................................................................................................
.......................................................................................................................
.......................................................................................................................
.......................................................................................................................
.......................................................................................................................

*'Thank you' is a wonderful phrase. Use it. It will add stature to your soul. — Marjorie Pay Hinckley*

## Daily Gratitude and Intention

Today I am grateful for:

...................................................................................
...................................................................................
...................................................................................
...................................................................................
...................................................................................
...................................................................................
...................................................................................
...................................................................................
...................................................................................
...................................................................................
...................................................................................
...................................................................................

Today's challenge and how it serves me to achieve my Life Priorities.

...................................................................................
...................................................................................
...................................................................................
...................................................................................
...................................................................................

My highest Intentions for Tomorrow:

...................................................................................
...................................................................................
...................................................................................
...................................................................................
...................................................................................

**OptimumThinking**.net

# AUG 15

## Daily Gratitude and Intention

Today I am grateful for:

..............................................................................................................................................
..............................................................................................................................................
..............................................................................................................................................
..............................................................................................................................................
..............................................................................................................................................
..............................................................................................................................................
..............................................................................................................................................
..............................................................................................................................................
..............................................................................................................................................
..............................................................................................................................................
..............................................................................................................................................
..............................................................................................................................................
..............................................................................................................................................
..............................................................................................................................................

Today's challenge and how it serves me to achieve my Life Priorities.

..............................................................................................................................................
..............................................................................................................................................
..............................................................................................................................................
..............................................................................................................................................
..............................................................................................................................................
..............................................................................................................................................

My highest Intentions for Tomorrow:

..............................................................................................................................................
..............................................................................................................................................
..............................................................................................................................................
..............................................................................................................................................
..............................................................................................................................................

*Thankfulness is the beginning of gratitude. Gratitude is the completion of thankfulness. Thankfulness may consist merely of words. Gratitude is shown in acts.*
*— Henri Frederic Amiel*

# Daily Gratitude and Intention

Today I am grateful for:

.................................................................................................
.................................................................................................
.................................................................................................
.................................................................................................
.................................................................................................
.................................................................................................
.................................................................................................
.................................................................................................
.................................................................................................
.................................................................................................
.................................................................................................

Today's challenge and how it serves me to achieve my Life Priorities.

.................................................................................................
.................................................................................................
.................................................................................................
.................................................................................................
.................................................................................................

My highest Intentions for Tomorrow:

.................................................................................................
.................................................................................................
.................................................................................................
.................................................................................................
.................................................................................................

# AUG 17

## Daily Gratitude and Intention

Today I am grateful for:

.................................................................................................................................
.................................................................................................................................
.................................................................................................................................
.................................................................................................................................
.................................................................................................................................
.................................................................................................................................
.................................................................................................................................
.................................................................................................................................
.................................................................................................................................
.................................................................................................................................
.................................................................................................................................
.................................................................................................................................
.................................................................................................................................

Today's challenge and how it serves me to achieve my Life Priorities.

.................................................................................................................................
.................................................................................................................................
.................................................................................................................................
.................................................................................................................................
.................................................................................................................................

My highest Intentions for Tomorrow:

.................................................................................................................................
.................................................................................................................................
.................................................................................................................................
.................................................................................................................................
.................................................................................................................................

## Daily Gratitude and Intention

Today I am grateful for:

........................................................................................................
........................................................................................................
........................................................................................................
........................................................................................................
........................................................................................................
........................................................................................................
........................................................................................................
........................................................................................................
........................................................................................................
........................................................................................................
........................................................................................................
........................................................................................................
........................................................................................................
........................................................................................................

Today's challenge and how it serves me to achieve my Life Priorities.

........................................................................................................
........................................................................................................
........................................................................................................
........................................................................................................
........................................................................................................

My highest Intentions for Tomorrow:

........................................................................................................
........................................................................................................
........................................................................................................
........................................................................................................
........................................................................................................

# AUG 19

## Daily Gratitude and Intention

Today I am grateful for:

..................................................................................................................
..................................................................................................................
..................................................................................................................
..................................................................................................................
..................................................................................................................
..................................................................................................................
..................................................................................................................
..................................................................................................................
..................................................................................................................
..................................................................................................................
..................................................................................................................
..................................................................................................................
..................................................................................................................

Today's challenge and how it serves me to achieve my Life Priorities.

..................................................................................................................
..................................................................................................................
..................................................................................................................
..................................................................................................................
..................................................................................................................
..................................................................................................................

My highest Intentions for Tomorrow:

..................................................................................................................
..................................................................................................................
..................................................................................................................
..................................................................................................................
..................................................................................................................

*Thanksgiving to God is an exuberant response to giving me HIS everything... by giving Him MY everything.*
*— Martha Kilpatrick*

# AUG 20

## Daily Gratitude and Intention

Today I am grateful for:

.......................................................................................................
.......................................................................................................
.......................................................................................................
.......................................................................................................
.......................................................................................................
.......................................................................................................
.......................................................................................................
.......................................................................................................
.......................................................................................................
.......................................................................................................
.......................................................................................................
.......................................................................................................
.......................................................................................................

Today's challenge and how it serves me to achieve my Life Priorities.

.......................................................................................................
.......................................................................................................
.......................................................................................................
.......................................................................................................
.......................................................................................................

My highest Intentions for Tomorrow:

.......................................................................................................
.......................................................................................................
.......................................................................................................
.......................................................................................................
.......................................................................................................

# AUG 21

*As many people as there are to hold you back, there are angels whose humanity makes up for all the others. I've had my share of angels. — Abraham Verghese*

## Daily Gratitude and Intention

Today I am grateful for:

..................................................................................................
..................................................................................................
..................................................................................................
..................................................................................................
..................................................................................................
..................................................................................................
..................................................................................................
..................................................................................................
..................................................................................................
..................................................................................................
..................................................................................................
..................................................................................................
..................................................................................................
..................................................................................................

Today's challenge and how it serves me to achieve my Life Priorities.

..................................................................................................
..................................................................................................
..................................................................................................
..................................................................................................
..................................................................................................

My highest Intentions for Tomorrow:

..................................................................................................
..................................................................................................
..................................................................................................
..................................................................................................
..................................................................................................

*That's what I learned. I learned I couldn't shed light on love other than to feel its comings and goings and be grateful. — Diane Keaton*

# AUG 22

## Daily Gratitude and Intention

Today I am grateful for:

..........................................................................................
..........................................................................................
..........................................................................................
..........................................................................................
..........................................................................................
..........................................................................................
..........................................................................................
..........................................................................................
..........................................................................................
..........................................................................................
..........................................................................................
..........................................................................................

Today's challenge and how it serves me to achieve my Life Priorities.

..........................................................................................
..........................................................................................
..........................................................................................
..........................................................................................
..........................................................................................

My highest Intentions for Tomorrow:

..........................................................................................
..........................................................................................
..........................................................................................
..........................................................................................
..........................................................................................

# AUG 23

*The best and most beautiful things in this world cannot be seen or even heard, but must be felt with the heart.*
*— Helen Keller*

## Daily Gratitude and Intention

Today I am grateful for:

..............................................................................................................................................................
..............................................................................................................................................................
..............................................................................................................................................................
..............................................................................................................................................................
..............................................................................................................................................................
..............................................................................................................................................................
..............................................................................................................................................................
..............................................................................................................................................................
..............................................................................................................................................................
..............................................................................................................................................................
..............................................................................................................................................................
..............................................................................................................................................................

Today's challenge and how it serves me to achieve my Life Priorities.

..............................................................................................................................................................
..............................................................................................................................................................
..............................................................................................................................................................
..............................................................................................................................................................
..............................................................................................................................................................

My highest Intentions for Tomorrow:

..............................................................................................................................................................
..............................................................................................................................................................
..............................................................................................................................................................
..............................................................................................................................................................
..............................................................................................................................................................

## Daily Gratitude and Intention

Today I am grateful for:

.............................................................................................................................
.............................................................................................................................
.............................................................................................................................
.............................................................................................................................
.............................................................................................................................
.............................................................................................................................
.............................................................................................................................
.............................................................................................................................
.............................................................................................................................
.............................................................................................................................
.............................................................................................................................
.............................................................................................................................

Today's challenge and how it serves me to achieve my Life Priorities.

.............................................................................................................................
.............................................................................................................................
.............................................................................................................................
.............................................................................................................................
.............................................................................................................................

My highest Intentions for Tomorrow:

.............................................................................................................................
.............................................................................................................................
.............................................................................................................................
.............................................................................................................................
.............................................................................................................................

# AUG 25

*The essence of all beautiful art, all great art, is gratitude. — Friedrich Nietzsche*

## Daily Gratitude and Intention

Today I am grateful for:

......................................................................................................
......................................................................................................
......................................................................................................
......................................................................................................
......................................................................................................
......................................................................................................
......................................................................................................
......................................................................................................
......................................................................................................
......................................................................................................
......................................................................................................
......................................................................................................
......................................................................................................
......................................................................................................

Today's challenge and how it serves me to achieve my Life Priorities.

......................................................................................................
......................................................................................................
......................................................................................................
......................................................................................................
......................................................................................................

My highest Intentions for Tomorrow:

......................................................................................................
......................................................................................................
......................................................................................................
......................................................................................................
......................................................................................................

*The grateful person, being still the most severe exacter of himself, not only confesses, but proclaims, his debts.*
*— Robert South*

# AUG 26

## Daily Gratitude and Intention

Today I am grateful for:

.......................................................................................................
.......................................................................................................
.......................................................................................................
.......................................................................................................
.......................................................................................................
.......................................................................................................
.......................................................................................................
.......................................................................................................
.......................................................................................................
.......................................................................................................
.......................................................................................................

Today's challenge and how it serves me to achieve my Life Priorities.

.......................................................................................................
.......................................................................................................
.......................................................................................................
.......................................................................................................
.......................................................................................................

My highest Intentions for Tomorrow:

.......................................................................................................
.......................................................................................................
.......................................................................................................
.......................................................................................................
.......................................................................................................

# AUG 27

## Daily Gratitude and Intention

Today I am grateful for:

..............................................................................................
..............................................................................................
..............................................................................................
..............................................................................................
..............................................................................................
..............................................................................................
..............................................................................................
..............................................................................................
..............................................................................................
..............................................................................................
..............................................................................................
..............................................................................................
..............................................................................................

Today's challenge and how it serves me to achieve my Life Priorities.

..............................................................................................
..............................................................................................
..............................................................................................
..............................................................................................
..............................................................................................

My highest Intentions for Tomorrow:

..............................................................................................
..............................................................................................
..............................................................................................
..............................................................................................
..............................................................................................

## Daily Gratitude and Intention

Today I am grateful for:

..............................................................................................
..............................................................................................
..............................................................................................
..............................................................................................
..............................................................................................
..............................................................................................
..............................................................................................
..............................................................................................
..............................................................................................
..............................................................................................
..............................................................................................
..............................................................................................
..............................................................................................

Today's challenge and how it serves me to achieve my Life Priorities.

..............................................................................................
..............................................................................................
..............................................................................................
..............................................................................................
..............................................................................................

My highest Intentions for Tomorrow:

..............................................................................................
..............................................................................................
..............................................................................................
..............................................................................................
..............................................................................................

# AUG 29

## Daily Gratitude and Intention

Today I am grateful for:

........................................................................
........................................................................
........................................................................
........................................................................
........................................................................
........................................................................
........................................................................
........................................................................
........................................................................
........................................................................
........................................................................
........................................................................
........................................................................
........................................................................
........................................................................

Today's challenge and how it serves me to achieve my Life Priorities.

........................................................................
........................................................................
........................................................................
........................................................................
........................................................................

My highest Intentions for Tomorrow:

........................................................................
........................................................................
........................................................................
........................................................................
........................................................................

*The miracle is not to walk on water. The miracle is to walk on the green earth, dwelling deeply in the present moment and feeling truly alive. — Thich Nhat Hanh*

## Daily Gratitude and Intention

Today I am grateful for:

.......................................................................
.......................................................................
.......................................................................
.......................................................................
.......................................................................
.......................................................................
.......................................................................
.......................................................................
.......................................................................
.......................................................................
.......................................................................
.......................................................................

Today's challenge and how it serves me to achieve my Life Priorities.

.......................................................................
.......................................................................
.......................................................................
.......................................................................
.......................................................................

My highest Intentions for Tomorrow:

.......................................................................
.......................................................................
.......................................................................
.......................................................................
.......................................................................

# AUG 31

*The moment one gives close attention to anything,
even a blade of grass, it becomes a mysterious,
awesome, indescribably magnificent world in itself.*
— *Henry Miller*

## Daily Gratitude and Intention

Today I am grateful for:

.......................................................................................................................
.......................................................................................................................
.......................................................................................................................
.......................................................................................................................
.......................................................................................................................
.......................................................................................................................
.......................................................................................................................
.......................................................................................................................
.......................................................................................................................
.......................................................................................................................
.......................................................................................................................
.......................................................................................................................
.......................................................................................................................

Today's challenge and how it serves me to achieve my Life Priorities.

.......................................................................................................................
.......................................................................................................................
.......................................................................................................................
.......................................................................................................................
.......................................................................................................................

My highest Intentions for Tomorrow:

.......................................................................................................................
.......................................................................................................................
.......................................................................................................................
.......................................................................................................................
.......................................................................................................................

Write it on your heart that
every day is the best day in the year.

— Ralph Waldo Emerson

# SEPTEMBER

## Monthly Intention Plan

Write the top priorities you intend to focus on in each area of your life during this month.

SPIRITUAL

......................................................................................................
......................................................................................................
......................................................................................................
......................................................................................................
......................................................................................................
......................................................................................................
......................................................................................................

MENTAL / EDUCATION

......................................................................................................
......................................................................................................
......................................................................................................
......................................................................................................
......................................................................................................
......................................................................................................
......................................................................................................

VOCATIONAL / CAREER

......................................................................................................
......................................................................................................
......................................................................................................
......................................................................................................
......................................................................................................
......................................................................................................
......................................................................................................

## FINANCIAL / SAVING & INVESTING

.............................................................................................................................................
.............................................................................................................................................
.............................................................................................................................................
.............................................................................................................................................
.............................................................................................................................................
.............................................................................................................................................
.............................................................................................................................................

## FAMILIAL / RELATIONSHIP

.............................................................................................................................................
.............................................................................................................................................
.............................................................................................................................................
.............................................................................................................................................
.............................................................................................................................................
.............................................................................................................................................
.............................................................................................................................................

## SOCIAL / FRIENDS

.............................................................................................................................................
.............................................................................................................................................
.............................................................................................................................................
.............................................................................................................................................
.............................................................................................................................................
.............................................................................................................................................
.............................................................................................................................................

## HEALTH & PHYSICAL APPEARANCE

.............................................................................................................................................
.............................................................................................................................................
.............................................................................................................................................
.............................................................................................................................................
.............................................................................................................................................
.............................................................................................................................................

# SEP 1

## Daily Gratitude and Intention

Today I am grateful for:

..................................................................................................
..................................................................................................
..................................................................................................
..................................................................................................
..................................................................................................
..................................................................................................
..................................................................................................
..................................................................................................
..................................................................................................
..................................................................................................
..................................................................................................
..................................................................................................
..................................................................................................
..................................................................................................

Today's challenge and how it serves me to achieve my Life Priorities.

..................................................................................................
..................................................................................................
..................................................................................................
..................................................................................................
..................................................................................................
..................................................................................................

My highest Intentions for Tomorrow:

..................................................................................................
..................................................................................................
..................................................................................................
..................................................................................................
..................................................................................................

The more we express our gratitude to God for our blessings, the more he will bring to our mind other blessings. The more we are aware of to be grateful for, the happier we become.
— Ezra Taft Benson

SEP 2

## Daily Gratitude and Intention

Today I am grateful for:

......................................................................................

......................................................................................

......................................................................................

......................................................................................

......................................................................................

......................................................................................

......................................................................................

......................................................................................

......................................................................................

......................................................................................

......................................................................................

......................................................................................

......................................................................................

Today's challenge and how it serves me to achieve my Life Priorities.

......................................................................................

......................................................................................

......................................................................................

......................................................................................

......................................................................................

My highest Intentions for Tomorrow:

......................................................................................

......................................................................................

......................................................................................

......................................................................................

......................................................................................

OptimumThinking.net

# SEP 3

## Daily Gratitude and Intention

Today I am grateful for:

.......................................................................................................................................
.......................................................................................................................................
.......................................................................................................................................
.......................................................................................................................................
.......................................................................................................................................
.......................................................................................................................................
.......................................................................................................................................
.......................................................................................................................................
.......................................................................................................................................
.......................................................................................................................................
.......................................................................................................................................
.......................................................................................................................................
.......................................................................................................................................

Today's challenge and how it serves me to achieve my Life Priorities.

.......................................................................................................................................
.......................................................................................................................................
.......................................................................................................................................
.......................................................................................................................................
.......................................................................................................................................

My highest Intentions for Tomorrow:

.......................................................................................................................................
.......................................................................................................................................
.......................................................................................................................................
.......................................................................................................................................
.......................................................................................................................................

*The more you recognize and express gratitude for the things you have, the more things you will have to express gratitude for.*
*— Zig Ziglar*

# SEP 4

## Daily Gratitude and Intention

Today I am grateful for:

.....................................................................................................................
.....................................................................................................................
.....................................................................................................................
.....................................................................................................................
.....................................................................................................................
.....................................................................................................................
.....................................................................................................................
.....................................................................................................................
.....................................................................................................................
.....................................................................................................................
.....................................................................................................................
.....................................................................................................................
.....................................................................................................................

Today's challenge and how it serves me to achieve my Life Priorities.

.....................................................................................................................
.....................................................................................................................
.....................................................................................................................
.....................................................................................................................
.....................................................................................................................
.....................................................................................................................

My highest Intentions for Tomorrow:

.....................................................................................................................
.....................................................................................................................
.....................................................................................................................
.....................................................................................................................
.....................................................................................................................
.....................................................................................................................

*The most important and most significant good quality in our human life is gratitude. — Sri Chinmoy*

## Daily Gratitude and Intention

Today I am grateful for:

..............................................................................
..............................................................................
..............................................................................
..............................................................................
..............................................................................
..............................................................................
..............................................................................
..............................................................................
..............................................................................
..............................................................................
..............................................................................
..............................................................................
..............................................................................
..............................................................................

Today's challenge and how it serves me to achieve my Life Priorities.

..............................................................................
..............................................................................
..............................................................................
..............................................................................
..............................................................................

My highest Intentions for Tomorrow:

..............................................................................
..............................................................................
..............................................................................
..............................................................................
..............................................................................

*The only people with whom you should try to get even are those who have helped you. — John E. Southard*

## Daily Gratitude and Intention

Today I am grateful for:

..........................................................................................
..........................................................................................
..........................................................................................
..........................................................................................
..........................................................................................
..........................................................................................
..........................................................................................
..........................................................................................
..........................................................................................
..........................................................................................
..........................................................................................
..........................................................................................
..........................................................................................

Today's challenge and how it serves me to achieve my Life Priorities.

..........................................................................................
..........................................................................................
..........................................................................................
..........................................................................................
..........................................................................................

My highest Intentions for Tomorrow:

..........................................................................................
..........................................................................................
..........................................................................................
..........................................................................................
..........................................................................................

# SEP 7

*The problem that we have with a victim mentality is that we forget to see the blessings of the day. Because of this, our spirit is poisoned instead of nourished. — Steve Maraboli*

## Daily Gratitude and Intention

Today I am grateful for:

........................................................................................................
........................................................................................................
........................................................................................................
........................................................................................................
........................................................................................................
........................................................................................................
........................................................................................................
........................................................................................................
........................................................................................................
........................................................................................................
........................................................................................................
........................................................................................................
........................................................................................................

Today's challenge and how it serves me to achieve my Life Priorities.

........................................................................................................
........................................................................................................
........................................................................................................
........................................................................................................
........................................................................................................

My highest Intentions for Tomorrow:

........................................................................................................
........................................................................................................
........................................................................................................
........................................................................................................
........................................................................................................

## Daily Gratitude and Intention

Today I am grateful for:

.......................................................................................................
.......................................................................................................
.......................................................................................................
.......................................................................................................
.......................................................................................................
.......................................................................................................
.......................................................................................................
.......................................................................................................
.......................................................................................................
.......................................................................................................
.......................................................................................................
.......................................................................................................
.......................................................................................................
.......................................................................................................

Today's challenge and how it serves me to achieve my Life Priorities.

.......................................................................................................
.......................................................................................................
.......................................................................................................
.......................................................................................................
.......................................................................................................

My highest Intentions for Tomorrow:

.......................................................................................................
.......................................................................................................
.......................................................................................................
.......................................................................................................
.......................................................................................................

# SEP 9

## Daily Gratitude and Intention

Today I am grateful for:

......................................................................................................................................
......................................................................................................................................
......................................................................................................................................
......................................................................................................................................
......................................................................................................................................
......................................................................................................................................
......................................................................................................................................
......................................................................................................................................
......................................................................................................................................
......................................................................................................................................
......................................................................................................................................
......................................................................................................................................

Today's challenge and how it serves me to achieve my Life Priorities.

......................................................................................................................................
......................................................................................................................................
......................................................................................................................................
......................................................................................................................................
......................................................................................................................................

My highest Intentions for Tomorrow:

......................................................................................................................................
......................................................................................................................................
......................................................................................................................................
......................................................................................................................................
......................................................................................................................................

*The unthankful heart...discovers no mercies; but let the thankful heart sweep through the day and, as the magnet finds the iron, so it will find, in every hour, some heavenly blessings! — Henry Ward Beecher*

# Daily Gratitude and Intention

Today I am grateful for:

.......................................................................................................................
.......................................................................................................................
.......................................................................................................................
.......................................................................................................................
.......................................................................................................................
.......................................................................................................................
.......................................................................................................................
.......................................................................................................................
.......................................................................................................................
.......................................................................................................................
.......................................................................................................................
.......................................................................................................................
.......................................................................................................................

Today's challenge and how it serves me to achieve my Life Priorities.

.......................................................................................................................
.......................................................................................................................
.......................................................................................................................
.......................................................................................................................
.......................................................................................................................

My highest Intentions for Tomorrow:

.......................................................................................................................
.......................................................................................................................
.......................................................................................................................
.......................................................................................................................
.......................................................................................................................
.......................................................................................................................

# SEP 11

*The world has enough beautiful mountains and meadows, spectacular skies and serene lakes. It has enough lush forests, flowered fields and sandy beaches. It has plenty of stars and the promise of a new sunrise and sunset every day. What the world needs more of is people to appreciate and enjoy it.* — Michael Josephson

## Daily Gratitude and Intention

Today I am grateful for:

........................................................................................

........................................................................................

........................................................................................

........................................................................................

........................................................................................

........................................................................................

........................................................................................

........................................................................................

........................................................................................

........................................................................................

........................................................................................

........................................................................................

Today's challenge and how it serves me to achieve my Life Priorities.

........................................................................................

........................................................................................

........................................................................................

........................................................................................

........................................................................................

My highest Intentions for Tomorrow:

........................................................................................

........................................................................................

........................................................................................

........................................................................................

........................................................................................

*The world is three days: As for yesterday it has vanished along with all that was in it. As for tomorrow you may never see it. As for today, it is yours, so work on it.*
*— Hasan Al-Basri*

# SEP 12

## Daily Gratitude and Intention

Today I am grateful for:

.............................................................................................
.............................................................................................
.............................................................................................
.............................................................................................
.............................................................................................
.............................................................................................
.............................................................................................
.............................................................................................
.............................................................................................
.............................................................................................
.............................................................................................
.............................................................................................

Today's challenge and how it serves me to achieve my Life Priorities.

.............................................................................................
.............................................................................................
.............................................................................................
.............................................................................................
.............................................................................................

My highest Intentions for Tomorrow:

.............................................................................................
.............................................................................................
.............................................................................................
.............................................................................................
.............................................................................................

# SEP 13

## Daily Gratitude and Intention

Today I am grateful for:

.................................................................................................
.................................................................................................
.................................................................................................
.................................................................................................
.................................................................................................
.................................................................................................
.................................................................................................
.................................................................................................
.................................................................................................
.................................................................................................
.................................................................................................
.................................................................................................
.................................................................................................

Today's challenge and how it serves me to achieve my Life Priorities.

.................................................................................................
.................................................................................................
.................................................................................................
.................................................................................................
.................................................................................................

My highest Intentions for Tomorrow:

.................................................................................................
.................................................................................................
.................................................................................................
.................................................................................................
.................................................................................................

*There is a calmness to a life lived in gratitude, a quiet joy. — Ralph H. Blum*

## Daily Gratitude and Intention

Today I am grateful for:

.....................................................................................................................................................
.....................................................................................................................................................
.....................................................................................................................................................
.....................................................................................................................................................
.....................................................................................................................................................
.....................................................................................................................................................
.....................................................................................................................................................
.....................................................................................................................................................
.....................................................................................................................................................
.....................................................................................................................................................
.....................................................................................................................................................
.....................................................................................................................................................
.....................................................................................................................................................
.....................................................................................................................................................

Today's challenge and how it serves me to achieve my Life Priorities.

.....................................................................................................................................................
.....................................................................................................................................................
.....................................................................................................................................................
.....................................................................................................................................................
.....................................................................................................................................................

My highest Intentions for Tomorrow:

.....................................................................................................................................................
.....................................................................................................................................................
.....................................................................................................................................................
.....................................................................................................................................................
.....................................................................................................................................................

# SEP 15

## Daily Gratitude and Intention

Today I am grateful for:

..........................................................................................
..........................................................................................
..........................................................................................
..........................................................................................
..........................................................................................
..........................................................................................
..........................................................................................
..........................................................................................
..........................................................................................
..........................................................................................
..........................................................................................
..........................................................................................
..........................................................................................
..........................................................................................

Today's challenge and how it serves me to achieve my Life Priorities.

..........................................................................................
..........................................................................................
..........................................................................................
..........................................................................................
..........................................................................................

My highest Intentions for Tomorrow:

..........................................................................................
..........................................................................................
..........................................................................................
..........................................................................................
..........................................................................................

*There is as much greatness of mind in acknowledging a good turn, as in doing it.*
*— Seneca*

# Daily Gratitude and Intention

Today I am grateful for:

.................................................................................................................
.................................................................................................................
.................................................................................................................
.................................................................................................................
.................................................................................................................
.................................................................................................................
.................................................................................................................
.................................................................................................................
.................................................................................................................
.................................................................................................................
.................................................................................................................
.................................................................................................................

Today's challenge and how it serves me to achieve my Life Priorities.

.................................................................................................................
.................................................................................................................
.................................................................................................................
.................................................................................................................
.................................................................................................................

My highest Intentions for Tomorrow:

.................................................................................................................
.................................................................................................................
.................................................................................................................
.................................................................................................................
.................................................................................................................

# SEP 17

## Daily Gratitude and Intention

Today I am grateful for:

.......................................................................................................................
.......................................................................................................................
.......................................................................................................................
.......................................................................................................................
.......................................................................................................................
.......................................................................................................................
.......................................................................................................................
.......................................................................................................................
.......................................................................................................................
.......................................................................................................................
.......................................................................................................................
.......................................................................................................................
.......................................................................................................................
.......................................................................................................................
.......................................................................................................................

Today's challenge and how it serves me to achieve my Life Priorities.

.......................................................................................................................
.......................................................................................................................
.......................................................................................................................
.......................................................................................................................
.......................................................................................................................
.......................................................................................................................

My highest Intentions for Tomorrow:

.......................................................................................................................
.......................................................................................................................
.......................................................................................................................
.......................................................................................................................
.......................................................................................................................

*There is no such thing as gratitude unexpressed. If it is unexpressed, it is plain, old-fashioned ingratitude.*
*— Robert Brault*

# SEP 18

## Daily Gratitude and Intention

Today I am grateful for:

....................................................................................................
....................................................................................................
....................................................................................................
....................................................................................................
....................................................................................................
....................................................................................................
....................................................................................................
....................................................................................................
....................................................................................................
....................................................................................................
....................................................................................................
....................................................................................................
....................................................................................................

Today's challenge and how it serves me to achieve my Life Priorities.

....................................................................................................
....................................................................................................
....................................................................................................
....................................................................................................
....................................................................................................

My highest Intentions for Tomorrow:

....................................................................................................
....................................................................................................
....................................................................................................
....................................................................................................
....................................................................................................

# SEP 19

## Daily Gratitude and Intention

Today I am grateful for:

.................................................................................
.................................................................................
.................................................................................
.................................................................................
.................................................................................
.................................................................................
.................................................................................
.................................................................................
.................................................................................
.................................................................................
.................................................................................
.................................................................................
.................................................................................
.................................................................................

Today's challenge and how it serves me to achieve my Life Priorities.

.................................................................................
.................................................................................
.................................................................................
.................................................................................
.................................................................................

My highest Intentions for Tomorrow:

.................................................................................
.................................................................................
.................................................................................
.................................................................................
.................................................................................

## Daily Gratitude and Intention

Today I am grateful for:

........................................................................................
........................................................................................
........................................................................................
........................................................................................
........................................................................................
........................................................................................
........................................................................................
........................................................................................
........................................................................................
........................................................................................
........................................................................................
........................................................................................
........................................................................................

Today's challenge and how it serves me to achieve my Life Priorities.

........................................................................................
........................................................................................
........................................................................................
........................................................................................
........................................................................................

My highest Intentions for Tomorrow:

........................................................................................
........................................................................................
........................................................................................
........................................................................................
........................................................................................

# SEP 21

There is only one thing that can form a bond between men, and that is gratitude...we cannot give someone else greater power over us than we have ourselves.
— Charles de Secondat

## Daily Gratitude and Intention

Today I am grateful for:

..............................................................................................................
..............................................................................................................
..............................................................................................................
..............................................................................................................
..............................................................................................................
..............................................................................................................
..............................................................................................................
..............................................................................................................
..............................................................................................................
..............................................................................................................
..............................................................................................................
..............................................................................................................

Today's challenge and how it serves me to achieve my Life Priorities.

..............................................................................................................
..............................................................................................................
..............................................................................................................
..............................................................................................................
..............................................................................................................

My highest Intentions for Tomorrow:

..............................................................................................................
..............................................................................................................
..............................................................................................................
..............................................................................................................
..............................................................................................................

## Daily Gratitude and Intention

Today I am grateful for:

..........................................................................................
..........................................................................................
..........................................................................................
..........................................................................................
..........................................................................................
..........................................................................................
..........................................................................................
..........................................................................................
..........................................................................................
..........................................................................................
..........................................................................................
..........................................................................................

Today's challenge and how it serves me to achieve my Life Priorities.

..........................................................................................
..........................................................................................
..........................................................................................
..........................................................................................
..........................................................................................
..........................................................................................

My highest Intentions for Tomorrow:

..........................................................................................
..........................................................................................
..........................................................................................
..........................................................................................
..........................................................................................
..........................................................................................

# SEP 23

## Daily Gratitude and Intention

Today I am grateful for:

..................................................................................................
..................................................................................................
..................................................................................................
..................................................................................................
..................................................................................................
..................................................................................................
..................................................................................................
..................................................................................................
..................................................................................................
..................................................................................................
..................................................................................................
..................................................................................................

Today's challenge and how it serves me to achieve my Life Priorities.

..................................................................................................
..................................................................................................
..................................................................................................
..................................................................................................
..................................................................................................

My highest Intentions for Tomorrow:

..................................................................................................
..................................................................................................
..................................................................................................
..................................................................................................
..................................................................................................

*Thou hast given so much to me, Give one thing more,—a grateful heart; Not thankful when it pleaseth me, As if Thy blessings had spare days, But such a heart whose pulse may be Thy praise. — George Herbert*

# SEP 24

## Daily Gratitude and Intention

Today I am grateful for:

.......................................................................................
.......................................................................................
.......................................................................................
.......................................................................................
.......................................................................................
.......................................................................................
.......................................................................................
.......................................................................................
.......................................................................................
.......................................................................................
.......................................................................................
.......................................................................................
.......................................................................................

Today's challenge and how it serves me to achieve my Life Priorities.

.......................................................................................
.......................................................................................
.......................................................................................
.......................................................................................
.......................................................................................

My highest Intentions for Tomorrow:

.......................................................................................
.......................................................................................
.......................................................................................
.......................................................................................
.......................................................................................

# SEP 25

## Daily Gratitude and Intention

Today I am grateful for:

......................................................................................................................................
......................................................................................................................................
......................................................................................................................................
......................................................................................................................................
......................................................................................................................................
......................................................................................................................................
......................................................................................................................................
......................................................................................................................................
......................................................................................................................................
......................................................................................................................................
......................................................................................................................................
......................................................................................................................................

Today's challenge and how it serves me to achieve my Life Priorities.

......................................................................................................................................
......................................................................................................................................
......................................................................................................................................
......................................................................................................................................
......................................................................................................................................

My highest Intentions for Tomorrow:

......................................................................................................................................
......................................................................................................................................
......................................................................................................................................
......................................................................................................................................
......................................................................................................................................

*To educate yourself for the feeling of gratitude means to take nothing for granted, but to always seek out and value the kind that will stand behind the action. Nothing that is done for you is a matter of course. Everything originates in a will for the good, which is directed at you. Train yourself never to put off the word or action for the expression of gratitude. — Albert Schweitzer*

# SEP 26

## Daily Gratitude and Intention

Today I am grateful for:

........................................................................
........................................................................
........................................................................
........................................................................
........................................................................
........................................................................
........................................................................
........................................................................
........................................................................
........................................................................
........................................................................
........................................................................
........................................................................
........................................................................

Today's challenge and how it serves me to achieve my Life Priorities.

........................................................................
........................................................................
........................................................................
........................................................................
........................................................................

My highest Intentions for Tomorrow:

........................................................................
........................................................................
........................................................................
........................................................................
........................................................................

# SEP 27

## Daily Gratitude and Intention

Today I am grateful for:

.................................................................................................................................
.................................................................................................................................
.................................................................................................................................
.................................................................................................................................
.................................................................................................................................
.................................................................................................................................
.................................................................................................................................
.................................................................................................................................
.................................................................................................................................
.................................................................................................................................
.................................................................................................................................
.................................................................................................................................
.................................................................................................................................

Today's challenge and how it serves me to achieve my Life Priorities.

.................................................................................................................................
.................................................................................................................................
.................................................................................................................................
.................................................................................................................................
.................................................................................................................................

My highest Intentions for Tomorrow:

.................................................................................................................................
.................................................................................................................................
.................................................................................................................................
.................................................................................................................................
.................................................................................................................................

*To speak gratitude is courteous and pleasant, to enact gratitude is generous and noble, but to live gratitude is to touch Heaven.* — *Johannes A. Gaertner*

## Daily Gratitude and Intention

Today I am grateful for:

..........................................................................................
..........................................................................................
..........................................................................................
..........................................................................................
..........................................................................................
..........................................................................................
..........................................................................................
..........................................................................................
..........................................................................................
..........................................................................................
..........................................................................................
..........................................................................................

Today's challenge and how it serves me to achieve my Life Priorities.

..........................................................................................
..........................................................................................
..........................................................................................
..........................................................................................
..........................................................................................

My highest Intentions for Tomorrow:

..........................................................................................
..........................................................................................
..........................................................................................
..........................................................................................
..........................................................................................

# SEP 29

*True forgiveness is when you can say,*
*"Thank you for that experience."*
*— Oprah Winfrey*

## Daily Gratitude and Intention

Today I am grateful for:

......................................................................................
......................................................................................
......................................................................................
......................................................................................
......................................................................................
......................................................................................
......................................................................................
......................................................................................
......................................................................................
......................................................................................
......................................................................................
......................................................................................
......................................................................................

Today's challenge and how it serves me to achieve my Life Priorities.

......................................................................................
......................................................................................
......................................................................................
......................................................................................
......................................................................................

My highest Intentions for Tomorrow:

......................................................................................
......................................................................................
......................................................................................
......................................................................................
......................................................................................

*True happiness is to enjoy the present, without anxious dependence upon the future, not to amuse ourselves with either hopes or fears but to rest satisfied with what we have, which is sufficient, for he that is so wants nothing.*
— Seneca

# SEP 30

## Daily Gratitude and Intention

Today I am grateful for:

........................................................................................................
........................................................................................................
........................................................................................................
........................................................................................................
........................................................................................................
........................................................................................................
........................................................................................................
........................................................................................................
........................................................................................................
........................................................................................................
........................................................................................................
........................................................................................................
........................................................................................................

Today's challenge and how it serves me to achieve my Life Priorities.

........................................................................................................
........................................................................................................
........................................................................................................
........................................................................................................
........................................................................................................

My highest Intentions for Tomorrow:

........................................................................................................
........................................................................................................
........................................................................................................
........................................................................................................
........................................................................................................

# OCTOBER

## Monthly Intention Plan

Write the top priorities you intend to focus on in each area of your life during this month.

SPIRITUAL

.................................................................................................................................
.................................................................................................................................
.................................................................................................................................
.................................................................................................................................
.................................................................................................................................
.................................................................................................................................
.................................................................................................................................

MENTAL / EDUCATION

.................................................................................................................................
.................................................................................................................................
.................................................................................................................................
.................................................................................................................................
.................................................................................................................................
.................................................................................................................................
.................................................................................................................................

VOCATIONAL / CAREER

.................................................................................................................................
.................................................................................................................................
.................................................................................................................................
.................................................................................................................................
.................................................................................................................................
.................................................................................................................................
.................................................................................................................................

## FINANCIAL / SAVING & INVESTING

..............................................................................................................................................
..............................................................................................................................................
..............................................................................................................................................
..............................................................................................................................................
..............................................................................................................................................
..............................................................................................................................................

## FAMILIAL / RELATIONSHIP

..............................................................................................................................................
..............................................................................................................................................
..............................................................................................................................................
..............................................................................................................................................
..............................................................................................................................................
..............................................................................................................................................

## SOCIAL / FRIENDS

..............................................................................................................................................
..............................................................................................................................................
..............................................................................................................................................
..............................................................................................................................................
..............................................................................................................................................
..............................................................................................................................................

## HEALTH & PHYSICAL APPEARANCE

..............................................................................................................................................
..............................................................................................................................................
..............................................................................................................................................
..............................................................................................................................................
..............................................................................................................................................
..............................................................................................................................................

# OCT 1

Two kinds of gratitude: The sudden kind we feel for
what we take; the larger kind we feel for what we give.
— Edwin Arlington Robinson

## Daily Gratitude and Intention

Today I am grateful for:

........................................................................................
........................................................................................
........................................................................................
........................................................................................
........................................................................................
........................................................................................
........................................................................................
........................................................................................
........................................................................................
........................................................................................
........................................................................................
........................................................................................

Today's challenge and how it serves me to achieve my Life Priorities.

........................................................................................
........................................................................................
........................................................................................
........................................................................................
........................................................................................

My highest Intentions for Tomorrow:

........................................................................................
........................................................................................
........................................................................................
........................................................................................

*Wake at dawn with a winged heart and*
*give thanks for another day of loving.*
*— Kahlil Gibran*

# OCT 2

## Daily Gratitude and Intention

Today I am grateful for:

..............................................................................................................................

..............................................................................................................................

..............................................................................................................................

..............................................................................................................................

..............................................................................................................................

..............................................................................................................................

..............................................................................................................................

..............................................................................................................................

..............................................................................................................................

..............................................................................................................................

..............................................................................................................................

..............................................................................................................................

Today's challenge and how it serves me to achieve my Life Priorities.

..............................................................................................................................

..............................................................................................................................

..............................................................................................................................

..............................................................................................................................

..............................................................................................................................

My highest Intentions for Tomorrow:

..............................................................................................................................

..............................................................................................................................

..............................................................................................................................

..............................................................................................................................

..............................................................................................................................

# OCT 3

## Daily Gratitude and Intention

Today I am grateful for:

..................................................................................................
..................................................................................................
..................................................................................................
..................................................................................................
..................................................................................................
..................................................................................................
..................................................................................................
..................................................................................................
..................................................................................................
..................................................................................................
..................................................................................................
..................................................................................................
..................................................................................................
..................................................................................................
..................................................................................................

Today's challenge and how it serves me to achieve my Life Priorities.

..................................................................................................
..................................................................................................
..................................................................................................
..................................................................................................
..................................................................................................

My highest Intentions for Tomorrow:

..................................................................................................
..................................................................................................
..................................................................................................
..................................................................................................
..................................................................................................

We are told that people stay in love because of chemistry, or because they remain intrigued with each other, because of many kindnesses, because of luck. But part of it has got to be forgiveness and gratefulness. — Ellen Goodman

# Daily Gratitude and Intention

Today I am grateful for:

...........................................................................................
...........................................................................................
...........................................................................................
...........................................................................................
...........................................................................................
...........................................................................................
...........................................................................................
...........................................................................................
...........................................................................................
...........................................................................................
...........................................................................................
...........................................................................................
...........................................................................................
...........................................................................................

Today's challenge and how it serves me to achieve my Life Priorities.

...........................................................................................
...........................................................................................
...........................................................................................
...........................................................................................
...........................................................................................

My highest Intentions for Tomorrow:

...........................................................................................
...........................................................................................
...........................................................................................
...........................................................................................
...........................................................................................

# OCT 5

We can only be said to be alive in those moments
when our hearts are conscious of our treasures.
— Thornton Wilder

## Daily Gratitude and Intention

Today I am grateful for:

Today's challenge and how it serves me to achieve my Life Priorities.

My highest Intentions for Tomorrow:

## Daily Gratitude and Intention

Today I am grateful for:

.......................................................................
.......................................................................
.......................................................................
.......................................................................
.......................................................................
.......................................................................
.......................................................................
.......................................................................
.......................................................................
.......................................................................
.......................................................................
.......................................................................
.......................................................................

Today's challenge and how it serves me to achieve my Life Priorities.

.......................................................................
.......................................................................
.......................................................................
.......................................................................
.......................................................................
.......................................................................

My highest Intentions for Tomorrow:

.......................................................................
.......................................................................
.......................................................................
.......................................................................
.......................................................................

# OCT 7

## Daily Gratitude and Intention

Today I am grateful for:

..............................................................................................................................
..............................................................................................................................
..............................................................................................................................
..............................................................................................................................
..............................................................................................................................
..............................................................................................................................
..............................................................................................................................
..............................................................................................................................
..............................................................................................................................
..............................................................................................................................
..............................................................................................................................
..............................................................................................................................

Today's challenge and how it serves me to achieve my Life Priorities.

..............................................................................................................................
..............................................................................................................................
..............................................................................................................................
..............................................................................................................................
..............................................................................................................................

My highest Intentions for Tomorrow:

..............................................................................................................................
..............................................................................................................................
..............................................................................................................................
..............................................................................................................................

We learned about gratitude and humility—that so many people had a hand in our success, from the teachers who inspired us to the janitors who kept our school clean…and we were taught to value everyone's contribution and treat everyone with respect.
— Michelle Obama

## Daily Gratitude and Intention

Today I am grateful for:

.......................................................................................................................
.......................................................................................................................
.......................................................................................................................
.......................................................................................................................
.......................................................................................................................
.......................................................................................................................
.......................................................................................................................
.......................................................................................................................
.......................................................................................................................
.......................................................................................................................
.......................................................................................................................
.......................................................................................................................
.......................................................................................................................
.......................................................................................................................

Today's challenge and how it serves me to achieve my Life Priorities.

.......................................................................................................................
.......................................................................................................................
.......................................................................................................................
.......................................................................................................................
.......................................................................................................................
.......................................................................................................................

My highest Intentions for Tomorrow:

.......................................................................................................................
.......................................................................................................................
.......................................................................................................................
.......................................................................................................................
.......................................................................................................................

OptimumThinking.net

# OCT 9

## Daily Gratitude and Intention

Today I am grateful for:

.......................................................................................................

.......................................................................................................

.......................................................................................................

.......................................................................................................

.......................................................................................................

.......................................................................................................

.......................................................................................................

.......................................................................................................

.......................................................................................................

.......................................................................................................

.......................................................................................................

.......................................................................................................

Today's challenge and how it serves me to achieve my Life Priorities.

.......................................................................................................

.......................................................................................................

.......................................................................................................

.......................................................................................................

.......................................................................................................

My highest Intentions for Tomorrow:

.......................................................................................................

.......................................................................................................

.......................................................................................................

.......................................................................................................

.......................................................................................................

## Daily Gratitude and Intention

Today I am grateful for:

.................................................................................................
.................................................................................................
.................................................................................................
.................................................................................................
.................................................................................................
.................................................................................................
.................................................................................................
.................................................................................................
.................................................................................................
.................................................................................................
.................................................................................................
.................................................................................................
.................................................................................................

Today's challenge and how it serves me to achieve my Life Priorities.

.................................................................................................
.................................................................................................
.................................................................................................
.................................................................................................
.................................................................................................

My highest Intentions for Tomorrow:

.................................................................................................
.................................................................................................
.................................................................................................
.................................................................................................
.................................................................................................

# OCT 11

## Daily Gratitude and Intention

Today I am grateful for:

.................................................................................................................
.................................................................................................................
.................................................................................................................
.................................................................................................................
.................................................................................................................
.................................................................................................................
.................................................................................................................
.................................................................................................................
.................................................................................................................
.................................................................................................................
.................................................................................................................
.................................................................................................................

Today's challenge and how it serves me to achieve my Life Priorities.

.................................................................................................................
.................................................................................................................
.................................................................................................................
.................................................................................................................
.................................................................................................................

My highest Intentions for Tomorrow:

.................................................................................................................
.................................................................................................................
.................................................................................................................
.................................................................................................................
.................................................................................................................

## Daily Gratitude and Intention

Today I am grateful for:

........................................................................
........................................................................
........................................................................
........................................................................
........................................................................
........................................................................
........................................................................
........................................................................
........................................................................
........................................................................
........................................................................
........................................................................
........................................................................

Today's challenge and how it serves me to achieve my Life Priorities.

........................................................................
........................................................................
........................................................................
........................................................................
........................................................................

My highest Intentions for Tomorrow:

........................................................................
........................................................................
........................................................................
........................................................................
........................................................................

# OCT 13

## Daily Gratitude and Intention

Today I am grateful for:

.......................................................................................................
.......................................................................................................
.......................................................................................................
.......................................................................................................
.......................................................................................................
.......................................................................................................
.......................................................................................................
.......................................................................................................
.......................................................................................................
.......................................................................................................
.......................................................................................................
.......................................................................................................

Today's challenge and how it serves me to achieve my Life Priorities.

.......................................................................................................
.......................................................................................................
.......................................................................................................
.......................................................................................................
.......................................................................................................

My highest Intentions for Tomorrow:

.......................................................................................................
.......................................................................................................
.......................................................................................................
.......................................................................................................
.......................................................................................................

*What if you gave someone a gift, and they neglected to thank you for it — would you be likely to give them another? Life is the same way. In order to attract more of the blessings that life has to offer, you must truly appreciate what you already have.*
— Ralph Marston

## Daily Gratitude and Intention

Today I am grateful for:

........................................................................................

........................................................................................

........................................................................................

........................................................................................

........................................................................................

........................................................................................

........................................................................................

........................................................................................

........................................................................................

........................................................................................

........................................................................................

........................................................................................

Today's challenge and how it serves me to achieve my Life Priorities.

........................................................................................

........................................................................................

........................................................................................

........................................................................................

My highest Intentions for Tomorrow:

........................................................................................

........................................................................................

........................................................................................

........................................................................................

........................................................................................

OptimumThinking.net

# OCT 15

## Daily Gratitude and Intention

Today I am grateful for:

...........................................................................................................................
...........................................................................................................................
...........................................................................................................................
...........................................................................................................................
...........................................................................................................................
...........................................................................................................................
...........................................................................................................................
...........................................................................................................................
...........................................................................................................................
...........................................................................................................................
...........................................................................................................................
...........................................................................................................................
...........................................................................................................................
...........................................................................................................................

Today's challenge and how it serves me to achieve my Life Priorities.

...........................................................................................................................
...........................................................................................................................
...........................................................................................................................
...........................................................................................................................
...........................................................................................................................

My highest Intentions for Tomorrow:

...........................................................................................................................
...........................................................................................................................
...........................................................................................................................
...........................................................................................................................
...........................................................................................................................

*Whatever our individual troubles and challenges may be, it's important to pause every now and then to appreciate all that we have, on every level. We need to literally "count our blessings," give thanks for them, allow ourselves to enjoy them, and relish the experience of prosperity we already have. — Shakti Gawain*

## Daily Gratitude and Intention

Today I am grateful for:

.................................................................................

.................................................................................

.................................................................................

.................................................................................

.................................................................................

.................................................................................

.................................................................................

.................................................................................

.................................................................................

.................................................................................

.................................................................................

Today's challenge and how it serves me to achieve my Life Priorities.

.................................................................................

.................................................................................

.................................................................................

.................................................................................

My highest Intentions for Tomorrow:

.................................................................................

.................................................................................

.................................................................................

.................................................................................

# OCT 17

*Whatever you appreciate and give thanks for will increase in your life.*
*— Sanaya Roman*

## Daily Gratitude and Intention

Today I am grateful for:

.............................................................................................
.............................................................................................
.............................................................................................
.............................................................................................
.............................................................................................
.............................................................................................
.............................................................................................
.............................................................................................
.............................................................................................
.............................................................................................
.............................................................................................
.............................................................................................
.............................................................................................

Today's challenge and how it serves me to achieve my Life Priorities.

.............................................................................................
.............................................................................................
.............................................................................................
.............................................................................................
.............................................................................................

My highest Intentions for Tomorrow:

.............................................................................................
.............................................................................................
.............................................................................................
.............................................................................................
.............................................................................................

*When eating bamboo sprouts,*
*remember the man who planted them.*
*— Chinese Proverb*

# OCT 18

## Daily Gratitude and Intention

Today I am grateful for:

..................................................................................................
..................................................................................................
..................................................................................................
..................................................................................................
..................................................................................................
..................................................................................................
..................................................................................................
..................................................................................................
..................................................................................................
..................................................................................................
..................................................................................................
..................................................................................................
..................................................................................................

Today's challenge and how it serves me to achieve my Life Priorities.

..................................................................................................
..................................................................................................
..................................................................................................
..................................................................................................
..................................................................................................

My highest Intentions for Tomorrow:

..................................................................................................
..................................................................................................
..................................................................................................
..................................................................................................
..................................................................................................

# OCT 19

## Daily Gratitude and Intention

Today I am grateful for:

..................................................................................................................................
..................................................................................................................................
..................................................................................................................................
..................................................................................................................................
..................................................................................................................................
..................................................................................................................................
..................................................................................................................................
..................................................................................................................................
..................................................................................................................................
..................................................................................................................................
..................................................................................................................................
..................................................................................................................................
..................................................................................................................................

Today's challenge and how it serves me to achieve my Life Priorities.

..................................................................................................................................
..................................................................................................................................
..................................................................................................................................
..................................................................................................................................
..................................................................................................................................

My highest Intentions for Tomorrow:

..................................................................................................................................
..................................................................................................................................
..................................................................................................................................
..................................................................................................................................
..................................................................................................................................

## Daily Gratitude and Intention

Today I am grateful for:

......................................................................................................
......................................................................................................
......................................................................................................
......................................................................................................
......................................................................................................
......................................................................................................
......................................................................................................
......................................................................................................
......................................................................................................
......................................................................................................
......................................................................................................
......................................................................................................
......................................................................................................

Today's challenge and how it serves me to achieve my Life Priorities.

......................................................................................................
......................................................................................................
......................................................................................................
......................................................................................................
......................................................................................................
......................................................................................................

My highest Intentions for Tomorrow:

......................................................................................................
......................................................................................................
......................................................................................................
......................................................................................................
......................................................................................................

# OCT 21

## Daily Gratitude and Intention

Today I am grateful for:

........................................................................................................
........................................................................................................
........................................................................................................
........................................................................................................
........................................................................................................
........................................................................................................
........................................................................................................
........................................................................................................
........................................................................................................
........................................................................................................
........................................................................................................
........................................................................................................
........................................................................................................

Today's challenge and how it serves me to achieve my Life Priorities.

........................................................................................................
........................................................................................................
........................................................................................................
........................................................................................................
........................................................................................................

My highest Intentions for Tomorrow:

........................................................................................................
........................................................................................................
........................................................................................................
........................................................................................................
........................................................................................................

When we become more fully aware that our success is due in large measure to the loyalty, helpfulness, and encouragement we have received from others, our desire grows to pass on similar gifts. Gratitude spurs us on to prove ourselves worthy of what others have done for us. The spirit of gratitude is a powerful energizer.
— Wilferd A. Peterson

## Daily Gratitude and Intention

Today I am grateful for:

....................................................................................

....................................................................................

....................................................................................

....................................................................................

....................................................................................

....................................................................................

....................................................................................

....................................................................................

....................................................................................

....................................................................................

Today's challenge and how it serves me to achieve my Life Priorities.

....................................................................................

....................................................................................

....................................................................................

....................................................................................

....................................................................................

My highest Intentions for Tomorrow:

....................................................................................

....................................................................................

....................................................................................

....................................................................................

....................................................................................

*When we give cheerfully and accept gratefully, everyone is blessed. — Maya Angelou*

## Daily Gratitude and Intention

Today I am grateful for:

...........................................................................................................................

...........................................................................................................................

...........................................................................................................................

...........................................................................................................................

...........................................................................................................................

...........................................................................................................................

...........................................................................................................................

...........................................................................................................................

...........................................................................................................................

...........................................................................................................................

...........................................................................................................................

...........................................................................................................................

Today's challenge and how it serves me to achieve my Life Priorities.

...........................................................................................................................

...........................................................................................................................

...........................................................................................................................

...........................................................................................................................

...........................................................................................................................

My highest Intentions for Tomorrow:

...........................................................................................................................

...........................................................................................................................

...........................................................................................................................

...........................................................................................................................

...........................................................................................................................

*When we replace a sense of service and gratitude with a sense of entitlement and expectation, we quickly see the demise of our relationships, society, and economy.*
— Steve Maraboli

## Daily Gratitude and Intention

Today I am grateful for:

.......................................................................................................
.......................................................................................................
.......................................................................................................
.......................................................................................................
.......................................................................................................
.......................................................................................................
.......................................................................................................
.......................................................................................................
.......................................................................................................
.......................................................................................................
.......................................................................................................
.......................................................................................................

Today's challenge and how it serves me to achieve my Life Priorities.

.......................................................................................................
.......................................................................................................
.......................................................................................................
.......................................................................................................
.......................................................................................................

My highest Intentions for Tomorrow:

.......................................................................................................
.......................................................................................................
.......................................................................................................
.......................................................................................................
.......................................................................................................

OptimumThinking.net

# OCT 25

## Daily Gratitude and Intention

Today I am grateful for:

..........................................................................................................
..........................................................................................................
..........................................................................................................
..........................................................................................................
..........................................................................................................
..........................................................................................................
..........................................................................................................
..........................................................................................................
..........................................................................................................
..........................................................................................................
..........................................................................................................
..........................................................................................................
..........................................................................................................

Today's challenge and how it serves me to achieve my Life Priorities.

..........................................................................................................
..........................................................................................................
..........................................................................................................
..........................................................................................................
..........................................................................................................

My highest Intentions for Tomorrow:

..........................................................................................................
..........................................................................................................
..........................................................................................................
..........................................................................................................

*When you are grateful fear disappears and abundance appears. — Tony Robbins*

## Daily Gratitude and Intention

Today I am grateful for:

.......................................................................................................

.......................................................................................................

.......................................................................................................

.......................................................................................................

.......................................................................................................

.......................................................................................................

.......................................................................................................

.......................................................................................................

.......................................................................................................

.......................................................................................................

.......................................................................................................

.......................................................................................................

Today's challenge and how it serves me to achieve my Life Priorities.

.......................................................................................................

.......................................................................................................

.......................................................................................................

.......................................................................................................

.......................................................................................................

My highest Intentions for Tomorrow:

.......................................................................................................

.......................................................................................................

.......................................................................................................

.......................................................................................................

.......................................................................................................

# OCT 27

*When you arise in the morning, think of what a precious privilege it is to be alive—to breathe, to think, to enjoy, to love—then make that day count! — Steve Maraboli*

## Daily Gratitude and Intention

Today I am grateful for:

.....................................................................................................
.....................................................................................................
.....................................................................................................
.....................................................................................................
.....................................................................................................
.....................................................................................................
.....................................................................................................
.....................................................................................................
.....................................................................................................
.....................................................................................................
.....................................................................................................
.....................................................................................................
.....................................................................................................

Today's challenge and how it serves me to achieve my Life Priorities.

.....................................................................................................
.....................................................................................................
.....................................................................................................
.....................................................................................................
.....................................................................................................

My highest Intentions for Tomorrow:

.....................................................................................................
.....................................................................................................
.....................................................................................................
.....................................................................................................
.....................................................................................................

*When you express gratitude for the blessings that come into your life, it not only encourages the universe to send you more, it also sees to it that those blessings remain.*
— Stephen Richards

## Daily Gratitude and Intention

Today I am grateful for:

....................................................................................
....................................................................................
....................................................................................
....................................................................................
....................................................................................
....................................................................................
....................................................................................
....................................................................................
....................................................................................
....................................................................................
....................................................................................
....................................................................................
....................................................................................
....................................................................................

Today's challenge and how it serves me to achieve my Life Priorities.

....................................................................................
....................................................................................
....................................................................................
....................................................................................
....................................................................................

My highest Intentions for Tomorrow:

....................................................................................
....................................................................................
....................................................................................
....................................................................................
....................................................................................

# OCT 29

Learn to remember you've got great friends, don't forget that and they will always care for you no matter what. Always remember to smile and look up at what you got in life. — Marilyn Monroe

## Daily Gratitude and Intention

Today I am grateful for:

.................................................................................................
.................................................................................................
.................................................................................................
.................................................................................................
.................................................................................................
.................................................................................................
.................................................................................................
.................................................................................................
.................................................................................................
.................................................................................................
.................................................................................................
.................................................................................................
.................................................................................................

Today's challenge and how it serves me to achieve my Life Priorities.

.................................................................................................
.................................................................................................
.................................................................................................
.................................................................................................
.................................................................................................
.................................................................................................

My highest Intentions for Tomorrow:

.................................................................................................
.................................................................................................
.................................................................................................
.................................................................................................
.................................................................................................

When your heart's gratitude comes to the fore, when you become all gratitude, this gratitude is like a flow, a flow of consciousness. It is always through gratitude that your consciousness-river will grow and water the perfection-tree inside you. — Sri Chinmoy

## Daily Gratitude and Intention

Today I am grateful for:

........................................................................................

........................................................................................

........................................................................................

........................................................................................

........................................................................................

........................................................................................

........................................................................................

........................................................................................

........................................................................................

........................................................................................

........................................................................................

........................................................................................

Today's challenge and how it serves me to achieve my Life Priorities.

........................................................................................

........................................................................................

........................................................................................

........................................................................................

My highest Intentions for Tomorrow:

........................................................................................

........................................................................................

........................................................................................

........................................................................................

# OCT 31

## Daily Gratitude and Intention

Today I am grateful for:

........................................................................................................
........................................................................................................
........................................................................................................
........................................................................................................
........................................................................................................
........................................................................................................
........................................................................................................
........................................................................................................
........................................................................................................
........................................................................................................
........................................................................................................
........................................................................................................

Today's challenge and how it serves me to achieve my Life Priorities.

........................................................................................................
........................................................................................................
........................................................................................................
........................................................................................................
........................................................................................................
........................................................................................................

My highest Intentions for Tomorrow:

........................................................................................................
........................................................................................................
........................................................................................................
........................................................................................................
........................................................................................................
........................................................................................................

Go confidently in the
direction of your dreams...
Live the life you've imagined.
— Thoreau

# NOVEMBER

## Monthly Intention Plan

Write the top priorities you intend to focus on in each area of your life during this month.

SPIRITUAL

........................................................................................
........................................................................................
........................................................................................
........................................................................................
........................................................................................
........................................................................................
........................................................................................

MENTAL / EDUCATION

........................................................................................
........................................................................................
........................................................................................
........................................................................................
........................................................................................
........................................................................................
........................................................................................

VOCATIONAL / CAREER

........................................................................................
........................................................................................
........................................................................................
........................................................................................
........................................................................................
........................................................................................
........................................................................................

## FINANCIAL / SAVING & INVESTING

......................................................................................................................................
......................................................................................................................................
......................................................................................................................................
......................................................................................................................................
......................................................................................................................................
......................................................................................................................................
......................................................................................................................................

## FAMILIAL / RELATIONSHIP

......................................................................................................................................
......................................................................................................................................
......................................................................................................................................
......................................................................................................................................
......................................................................................................................................
......................................................................................................................................
......................................................................................................................................
......................................................................................................................................

## SOCIAL / FRIENDS

......................................................................................................................................
......................................................................................................................................
......................................................................................................................................
......................................................................................................................................
......................................................................................................................................
......................................................................................................................................
......................................................................................................................................
......................................................................................................................................

## HEALTH & PHYSICAL APPEARANCE

......................................................................................................................................
......................................................................................................................................
......................................................................................................................................
......................................................................................................................................
......................................................................................................................................
......................................................................................................................................

# NOV 1

*Whenever we have thanked these men and women for what they have done for us, without exception they have expressed gratitude for having the chance to help—because they grew as they served.*
*— Clayton Christensen*

## Daily Gratitude and Intention

Today I am grateful for:

.................................................................................................................................
.................................................................................................................................
.................................................................................................................................
.................................................................................................................................
.................................................................................................................................
.................................................................................................................................
.................................................................................................................................
.................................................................................................................................
.................................................................................................................................
.................................................................................................................................
.................................................................................................................................

Today's challenge and how it serves me to achieve my Life Priorities.

.................................................................................................................................
.................................................................................................................................
.................................................................................................................................
.................................................................................................................................
.................................................................................................................................

My highest Intentions for Tomorrow:

.................................................................................................................................
.................................................................................................................................
.................................................................................................................................
.................................................................................................................................
.................................................................................................................................

*Wherever I have knocked, a door has opened.*
*Wherever I have wandered, a path has appeared.*
*— Alice Walker*

## Daily Gratitude and Intention

Today I am grateful for:

.................................................................................
.................................................................................
.................................................................................
.................................................................................
.................................................................................
.................................................................................
.................................................................................
.................................................................................
.................................................................................
.................................................................................
.................................................................................
.................................................................................
.................................................................................
.................................................................................

Today's challenge and how it serves me to achieve my Life Priorities.

.................................................................................
.................................................................................
.................................................................................
.................................................................................
.................................................................................

My highest Intentions for Tomorrow:

.................................................................................
.................................................................................
.................................................................................
.................................................................................
.................................................................................

OptimumThinking.net

# NOV 3

*Who does not thank for little will not thank for much.*
*— Estonian Proverb*

## Daily Gratitude and Intention

Today I am grateful for:

.............................................................................................................................
.............................................................................................................................
.............................................................................................................................
.............................................................................................................................
.............................................................................................................................
.............................................................................................................................
.............................................................................................................................
.............................................................................................................................
.............................................................................................................................
.............................................................................................................................
.............................................................................................................................
.............................................................................................................................
.............................................................................................................................

Today's challenge and how it serves me to achieve my Life Priorities.

.............................................................................................................................
.............................................................................................................................
.............................................................................................................................
.............................................................................................................................
.............................................................................................................................

My highest Intentions for Tomorrow:

.............................................................................................................................
.............................................................................................................................
.............................................................................................................................
.............................................................................................................................
.............................................................................................................................

*With arms outstretched I thank. With heart beating gratefully
I love. With body in health I jump for joy. With spirit full I live.
— Terri Guillemets*

## Daily Gratitude and Intention

Today I am grateful for:

.................................................................................................
.................................................................................................
.................................................................................................
.................................................................................................
.................................................................................................
.................................................................................................
.................................................................................................
.................................................................................................
.................................................................................................
.................................................................................................
.................................................................................................
.................................................................................................
.................................................................................................
.................................................................................................

Today's challenge and how it serves me to achieve my Life Priorities.

.................................................................................................
.................................................................................................
.................................................................................................
.................................................................................................
.................................................................................................

My highest Intentions for Tomorrow:

.................................................................................................
.................................................................................................
.................................................................................................
.................................................................................................
.................................................................................................

# NOV 5

## Daily Gratitude and Intention

Today I am grateful for:

........................................................................................

........................................................................................

........................................................................................

........................................................................................

........................................................................................

........................................................................................

........................................................................................

........................................................................................

........................................................................................

........................................................................................

........................................................................................

Today's challenge and how it serves me to achieve my Life Priorities.

........................................................................................

........................................................................................

........................................................................................

........................................................................................

........................................................................................

My highest Intentions for Tomorrow:

........................................................................................

........................................................................................

........................................................................................

........................................................................................

........................................................................................

You say grace before meals. All right. But I say grace before
the concert and the opera, and grace before the play and
pantomime, and grace before I open a book, and grace before
sketching, painting, swimming, fencing, boxing, walking, playing,
dancing and grace before I dip the pen in the ink.
— G. K. Chesterton

## Daily Gratitude and Intention

Today I am grateful for:

.......................................................................................................................
.......................................................................................................................
.......................................................................................................................
.......................................................................................................................
.......................................................................................................................
.......................................................................................................................
.......................................................................................................................
.......................................................................................................................
.......................................................................................................................
.......................................................................................................................
.......................................................................................................................
.......................................................................................................................
.......................................................................................................................

Today's challenge and how it serves me to achieve my Life Priorities.

.......................................................................................................................
.......................................................................................................................
.......................................................................................................................
.......................................................................................................................
.......................................................................................................................

My highest Intentions for Tomorrow:

.......................................................................................................................
.......................................................................................................................
.......................................................................................................................
.......................................................................................................................
.......................................................................................................................

# NOV 7

You say, 'If I had a little more, I should be very satisfied.'
You make a mistake. If you are not content with what you
have, you would not be satisfied if it were doubled.
— Charles Haddon Spurgeon

## Daily Gratitude and Intention

Today I am grateful for:

.......................................................................................................
.......................................................................................................
.......................................................................................................
.......................................................................................................
.......................................................................................................
.......................................................................................................
.......................................................................................................
.......................................................................................................
.......................................................................................................
.......................................................................................................
.......................................................................................................
.......................................................................................................
.......................................................................................................

Today's challenge and how it serves me to achieve my Life Priorities.

.......................................................................................................
.......................................................................................................
.......................................................................................................
.......................................................................................................
.......................................................................................................

My highest Intentions for Tomorrow:

.......................................................................................................
.......................................................................................................
.......................................................................................................
.......................................................................................................
.......................................................................................................

You simply will not be the same person two months from now after consciously giving thanks each day for the abundance that exists in your life. And you will have set in motion an ancient spiritual law: the more you have and are grateful for, the more will be given you. — Sarah Ban Breathnach

## Daily Gratitude and Intention

Today I am grateful for:

.........................................................................................
.........................................................................................
.........................................................................................
.........................................................................................
.........................................................................................
.........................................................................................
.........................................................................................
.........................................................................................
.........................................................................................
.........................................................................................
.........................................................................................
.........................................................................................
.........................................................................................
.........................................................................................

Today's challenge and how it serves me to achieve my Life Priorities.

.........................................................................................
.........................................................................................
.........................................................................................
.........................................................................................
.........................................................................................

My highest Intentions for Tomorrow:

.........................................................................................
.........................................................................................
.........................................................................................
.........................................................................................
.........................................................................................

# NOV 9

*Expressing our gratitude helps us appreciate that we truly are already living our life purpose every day.*

## Daily Gratitude and Intention

Today I am grateful for:

........................................................................................

........................................................................................

........................................................................................

........................................................................................

........................................................................................

........................................................................................

........................................................................................

........................................................................................

........................................................................................

........................................................................................

........................................................................................

........................................................................................

........................................................................................

........................................................................................

Today's challenge and how it serves me to achieve my Life Priorities.

........................................................................................

........................................................................................

........................................................................................

........................................................................................

........................................................................................

........................................................................................

My highest Intentions for Tomorrow:

........................................................................................

........................................................................................

........................................................................................

........................................................................................

........................................................................................

Take the time to clarify your life purpose to yourself clearly so that you can consciously create the life you choose. There is only one person who gets up each day and dedicates their life to living your dream!

## Daily Gratitude and Intention

Today I am grateful for:

........................................................................................
........................................................................................
........................................................................................
........................................................................................
........................................................................................
........................................................................................
........................................................................................
........................................................................................
........................................................................................
........................................................................................
........................................................................................
........................................................................................

Today's challenge and how it serves me to achieve my Life Priorities.

........................................................................................
........................................................................................
........................................................................................
........................................................................................
........................................................................................

My highest Intentions for Tomorrow:

........................................................................................
........................................................................................
........................................................................................
........................................................................................
........................................................................................

**Optimum**Thinking.net

# NOV 11

*If you don't get what you want, it is a sign that either you did not seriously want it, or that you tried to bargain over the price. — Rudyard Kipling*

## Daily Gratitude and Intention

Today I am grateful for:

........................................................................................................

........................................................................................................

........................................................................................................

........................................................................................................

........................................................................................................

........................................................................................................

........................................................................................................

........................................................................................................

........................................................................................................

........................................................................................................

........................................................................................................

........................................................................................................

........................................................................................................

........................................................................................................

Today's challenge and how it serves me to achieve my Life Priorities.

........................................................................................................

........................................................................................................

........................................................................................................

........................................................................................................

........................................................................................................

My highest Intentions for Tomorrow:

........................................................................................................

........................................................................................................

........................................................................................................

........................................................................................................

........................................................................................................

*You already have everything your heart desires.*
*— Traditional proverb*

## Daily Gratitude and Intention

Today I am grateful for:

..................................................................................................
..................................................................................................
..................................................................................................
..................................................................................................
..................................................................................................
..................................................................................................
..................................................................................................
..................................................................................................
..................................................................................................
..................................................................................................
..................................................................................................
..................................................................................................
..................................................................................................

Today's challenge and how it serves me to achieve my Life Priorities.

..................................................................................................
..................................................................................................
..................................................................................................
..................................................................................................
..................................................................................................

My highest Intentions for Tomorrow:

..................................................................................................
..................................................................................................
..................................................................................................
..................................................................................................
..................................................................................................

# NOV 13

*Many of us spend half our time wishing for things that we could have if we didn't spend half our time wishing.*
*— Alexander Woollcott*

## Daily Gratitude and Intention

Today I am grateful for:

..................................................................................................
..................................................................................................
..................................................................................................
..................................................................................................
..................................................................................................
..................................................................................................
..................................................................................................
..................................................................................................
..................................................................................................
..................................................................................................
..................................................................................................
..................................................................................................

Today's challenge and how it serves me to achieve my Life Priorities.

..................................................................................................
..................................................................................................
..................................................................................................
..................................................................................................
..................................................................................................

My highest Intentions for Tomorrow:

..................................................................................................
..................................................................................................
..................................................................................................
..................................................................................................
..................................................................................................

## Daily Gratitude and Intention

Today I am grateful for:

..............................................................................................................
..............................................................................................................
..............................................................................................................
..............................................................................................................
..............................................................................................................
..............................................................................................................
..............................................................................................................
..............................................................................................................
..............................................................................................................
..............................................................................................................
..............................................................................................................
..............................................................................................................
..............................................................................................................
..............................................................................................................
..............................................................................................................

Today's challenge and how it serves me to achieve my Life Priorities.

..............................................................................................................
..............................................................................................................
..............................................................................................................
..............................................................................................................
..............................................................................................................

My highest Intentions for Tomorrow:

..............................................................................................................
..............................................................................................................
..............................................................................................................
..............................................................................................................

# NOV 15

*Circumstances may be likened to stones — you can use them to build with, or you can let them weigh you down.*
*— John Demartini*

## Daily Gratitude and Intention

Today I am grateful for:

........................................................................................

........................................................................................

........................................................................................

........................................................................................

........................................................................................

........................................................................................

........................................................................................

........................................................................................

........................................................................................

........................................................................................

........................................................................................

........................................................................................

Today's challenge and how it serves me to achieve my Life Priorities.

........................................................................................

........................................................................................

........................................................................................

........................................................................................

........................................................................................

My highest Intentions for Tomorrow:

........................................................................................

........................................................................................

........................................................................................

........................................................................................

........................................................................................

## Daily Gratitude and Intention

Today I am grateful for:

.................................................................................................
.................................................................................................
.................................................................................................
.................................................................................................
.................................................................................................
.................................................................................................
.................................................................................................
.................................................................................................
.................................................................................................
.................................................................................................
.................................................................................................
.................................................................................................
.................................................................................................

Today's challenge and how it serves me to achieve my Life Priorities.

.................................................................................................
.................................................................................................
.................................................................................................
.................................................................................................
.................................................................................................
.................................................................................................

My highest Intentions for Tomorrow:

.................................................................................................
.................................................................................................
.................................................................................................
.................................................................................................
.................................................................................................

# NOV 17

## Daily Gratitude and Intention

Today I am grateful for:

.......................................................................................................
.......................................................................................................
.......................................................................................................
.......................................................................................................
.......................................................................................................
.......................................................................................................
.......................................................................................................
.......................................................................................................
.......................................................................................................
.......................................................................................................
.......................................................................................................
.......................................................................................................
.......................................................................................................
.......................................................................................................
.......................................................................................................

Today's challenge and how it serves me to achieve my Life Priorities.

.......................................................................................................
.......................................................................................................
.......................................................................................................
.......................................................................................................
.......................................................................................................

My highest Intentions for Tomorrow:

.......................................................................................................
.......................................................................................................
.......................................................................................................
.......................................................................................................

## Daily Gratitude and Intention

Today I am grateful for:

........................................................................................................................................
........................................................................................................................................
........................................................................................................................................
........................................................................................................................................
........................................................................................................................................
........................................................................................................................................
........................................................................................................................................
........................................................................................................................................
........................................................................................................................................
........................................................................................................................................
........................................................................................................................................
........................................................................................................................................

Today's challenge and how it serves me to achieve my Life Priorities.

........................................................................................................................................
........................................................................................................................................
........................................................................................................................................
........................................................................................................................................
........................................................................................................................................

My highest Intentions for Tomorrow:

........................................................................................................................................
........................................................................................................................................
........................................................................................................................................
........................................................................................................................................
........................................................................................................................................

# NOV 19

*If you haven't got all the things you want, be grateful for the things you don't have that you don't want.*
*— Anonymous*

## Daily Gratitude and Intention

Today I am grateful for:

.......................................................................................................
.......................................................................................................
.......................................................................................................
.......................................................................................................
.......................................................................................................
.......................................................................................................
.......................................................................................................
.......................................................................................................
.......................................................................................................
.......................................................................................................
.......................................................................................................
.......................................................................................................

Today's challenge and how it serves me to achieve my Life Priorities.

.......................................................................................................
.......................................................................................................
.......................................................................................................
.......................................................................................................
.......................................................................................................

My highest Intentions for Tomorrow:

.......................................................................................................
.......................................................................................................
.......................................................................................................
.......................................................................................................

*When you thank yourself and others, you open your heart to inspiration. — John Demartini*

## Daily Gratitude and Intention

Today I am grateful for:

........................................................................................................................

........................................................................................................................

........................................................................................................................

........................................................................................................................

........................................................................................................................

........................................................................................................................

........................................................................................................................

........................................................................................................................

........................................................................................................................

........................................................................................................................

........................................................................................................................

........................................................................................................................

........................................................................................................................

........................................................................................................................

Today's challenge and how it serves me to achieve my Life Priorities.

........................................................................................................................

........................................................................................................................

........................................................................................................................

........................................................................................................................

........................................................................................................................

........................................................................................................................

My highest Intentions for Tomorrow:

........................................................................................................................

........................................................................................................................

........................................................................................................................

........................................................................................................................

........................................................................................................................

# NOV 21

*Energy and vitality are infinite when you recognize and appreciate their source: a heart filled with gratitude.*
*— John Demartini*

## Daily Gratitude and Intention

Today I am grateful for:

.....................................................................................................................................................
.....................................................................................................................................................
.....................................................................................................................................................
.....................................................................................................................................................
.....................................................................................................................................................
.....................................................................................................................................................
.....................................................................................................................................................
.....................................................................................................................................................
.....................................................................................................................................................
.....................................................................................................................................................
.....................................................................................................................................................
.....................................................................................................................................................
.....................................................................................................................................................
.....................................................................................................................................................

Today's challenge and how it serves me to achieve my Life Priorities.

.....................................................................................................................................................
.....................................................................................................................................................
.....................................................................................................................................................
.....................................................................................................................................................
.....................................................................................................................................................
.....................................................................................................................................................

My highest Intentions for Tomorrow:

.....................................................................................................................................................
.....................................................................................................................................................
.....................................................................................................................................................
.....................................................................................................................................................
.....................................................................................................................................................
.....................................................................................................................................................

*Inspiration is everywhere. If you're ready to appreciate it, an ant can be one of the wonders of the world.*
*— Anonymous*

## Daily Gratitude and Intention

Today I am grateful for:

..................................................................................................................
..................................................................................................................
..................................................................................................................
..................................................................................................................
..................................................................................................................
..................................................................................................................
..................................................................................................................
..................................................................................................................
..................................................................................................................
..................................................................................................................
..................................................................................................................
..................................................................................................................
..................................................................................................................
..................................................................................................................

Today's challenge and how it serves me to achieve my Life Priorities.

..................................................................................................................
..................................................................................................................
..................................................................................................................
..................................................................................................................
..................................................................................................................

My highest Intentions for Tomorrow:

..................................................................................................................
..................................................................................................................
..................................................................................................................
..................................................................................................................
..................................................................................................................

# NOV 23

*Inspiring messages are available at every moment;*
*just be truly grateful and listen with your heart.*
*— John Demartini*

## Daily Gratitude and Intention

Today I am grateful for:

......................................................................................................

......................................................................................................

......................................................................................................

......................................................................................................

......................................................................................................

......................................................................................................

......................................................................................................

......................................................................................................

......................................................................................................

......................................................................................................

......................................................................................................

......................................................................................................

......................................................................................................

Today's challenge and how it serves me to achieve my Life Priorities.

......................................................................................................

......................................................................................................

......................................................................................................

......................................................................................................

......................................................................................................

My highest Intentions for Tomorrow:

......................................................................................................

......................................................................................................

......................................................................................................

......................................................................................................

......................................................................................................

## Daily Gratitude and Intention

Today I am grateful for:

....................................................................................................
....................................................................................................
....................................................................................................
....................................................................................................
....................................................................................................
....................................................................................................
....................................................................................................
....................................................................................................
....................................................................................................
....................................................................................................
....................................................................................................
....................................................................................................
....................................................................................................

Today's challenge and how it serves me to achieve my Life Priorities.

....................................................................................................
....................................................................................................
....................................................................................................
....................................................................................................
....................................................................................................

My highest Intentions for Tomorrow:

....................................................................................................
....................................................................................................
....................................................................................................
....................................................................................................
....................................................................................................

# NOV 25

## Daily Gratitude and Intention

Today I am grateful for:

........................................................................................................
........................................................................................................
........................................................................................................
........................................................................................................
........................................................................................................
........................................................................................................
........................................................................................................
........................................................................................................
........................................................................................................
........................................................................................................
........................................................................................................
........................................................................................................
........................................................................................................

Today's challenge and how it serves me to achieve my Life Priorities.

........................................................................................................
........................................................................................................
........................................................................................................
........................................................................................................
........................................................................................................
........................................................................................................

My highest Intentions for Tomorrow:

........................................................................................................
........................................................................................................
........................................................................................................
........................................................................................................
........................................................................................................

*It is not love, but lack of love, which is blind.*
*— Glenway Westcott*

## Daily Gratitude and Intention

Today I am grateful for:

.....................................................................................................
.....................................................................................................
.....................................................................................................
.....................................................................................................
.....................................................................................................
.....................................................................................................
.....................................................................................................
.....................................................................................................
.....................................................................................................
.....................................................................................................
.....................................................................................................
.....................................................................................................
.....................................................................................................
.....................................................................................................

Today's challenge and how it serves me to achieve my Life Priorities.

.....................................................................................................
.....................................................................................................
.....................................................................................................
.....................................................................................................
.....................................................................................................

My highest Intentions for Tomorrow:

.....................................................................................................
.....................................................................................................
.....................................................................................................
.....................................................................................................
.....................................................................................................

# NOV 27

## Daily Gratitude and Intention

Today I am grateful for:

Today's challenge and how it serves me to achieve my Life Priorities.

My highest Intentions for Tomorrow:

*Since our mission is to discover what we don't love and learn to love it, the people who get on our nerves most are among our greatest teachers! — John Demartini*

## Daily Gratitude and Intention

Today I am grateful for:

.......................................................................................................................
.......................................................................................................................
.......................................................................................................................
.......................................................................................................................
.......................................................................................................................
.......................................................................................................................
.......................................................................................................................
.......................................................................................................................
.......................................................................................................................
.......................................................................................................................
.......................................................................................................................
.......................................................................................................................
.......................................................................................................................
.......................................................................................................................
.......................................................................................................................

Today's challenge and how it serves me to achieve my Life Priorities.

.......................................................................................................................
.......................................................................................................................
.......................................................................................................................
.......................................................................................................................
.......................................................................................................................
.......................................................................................................................

My highest Intentions for Tomorrow:

.......................................................................................................................
.......................................................................................................................
.......................................................................................................................
.......................................................................................................................
.......................................................................................................................
.......................................................................................................................

# NOV 29

## Daily Gratitude and Intention

Today I am grateful for:

.................................................................................................
.................................................................................................
.................................................................................................
.................................................................................................
.................................................................................................
.................................................................................................
.................................................................................................
.................................................................................................
.................................................................................................
.................................................................................................
.................................................................................................
.................................................................................................

Today's challenge and how it serves me to achieve my Life Priorities.

.................................................................................................
.................................................................................................
.................................................................................................
.................................................................................................
.................................................................................................

My highest Intentions for Tomorrow:

.................................................................................................
.................................................................................................
.................................................................................................
.................................................................................................
.................................................................................................

*Basically my wife was immature. I'd be at home in the bath and she'd come in and sink my boats.*
*— Woody Allen*

## Daily Gratitude and Intention

Today I am grateful for:

..................................................................................................................
..................................................................................................................
..................................................................................................................
..................................................................................................................
..................................................................................................................
..................................................................................................................
..................................................................................................................
..................................................................................................................
..................................................................................................................
..................................................................................................................
..................................................................................................................
..................................................................................................................
..................................................................................................................
..................................................................................................................
..................................................................................................................
..................................................................................................................

Today's challenge and how it serves me to achieve my Life Priorities.

..................................................................................................................
..................................................................................................................
..................................................................................................................
..................................................................................................................
..................................................................................................................
..................................................................................................................

My highest Intentions for Tomorrow:

..................................................................................................................
..................................................................................................................
..................................................................................................................
..................................................................................................................
..................................................................................................................

# DECEMBER

## Monthly Intention Plan

Write the top priorities you intend to focus on in each area of your life during this month.

SPIRITUAL

...............................................................................................................................................................
...............................................................................................................................................................
...............................................................................................................................................................
...............................................................................................................................................................
...............................................................................................................................................................
...............................................................................................................................................................
...............................................................................................................................................................
...............................................................................................................................................................

MENTAL / EDUCATION

...............................................................................................................................................................
...............................................................................................................................................................
...............................................................................................................................................................
...............................................................................................................................................................
...............................................................................................................................................................
...............................................................................................................................................................
...............................................................................................................................................................
...............................................................................................................................................................

VOCATIONAL / CAREER

...............................................................................................................................................................
...............................................................................................................................................................
...............................................................................................................................................................
...............................................................................................................................................................
...............................................................................................................................................................
...............................................................................................................................................................
...............................................................................................................................................................
...............................................................................................................................................................

## FINANCIAL / SAVING & INVESTING

........................................................................................................

........................................................................................................

........................................................................................................

........................................................................................................

........................................................................................................

........................................................................................................

........................................................................................................

## FAMILIAL / RELATIONSHIP

........................................................................................................

........................................................................................................

........................................................................................................

........................................................................................................

........................................................................................................

........................................................................................................

........................................................................................................

## SOCIAL / FRIENDS

........................................................................................................

........................................................................................................

........................................................................................................

........................................................................................................

........................................................................................................

........................................................................................................

........................................................................................................

## HEALTH & PHYSICAL APPEARANCE

........................................................................................................

........................................................................................................

........................................................................................................

........................................................................................................

........................................................................................................

........................................................................................................

........................................................................................................

# DEC 1

## Daily Gratitude and Intention

Today I am grateful for:

..................................................................................................................
..................................................................................................................
..................................................................................................................
..................................................................................................................
..................................................................................................................
..................................................................................................................
..................................................................................................................
..................................................................................................................
..................................................................................................................
..................................................................................................................
..................................................................................................................
..................................................................................................................
..................................................................................................................

Today's challenge and how it serves me to achieve my Life Priorities.

..................................................................................................................
..................................................................................................................
..................................................................................................................
..................................................................................................................
..................................................................................................................

My highest Intentions for Tomorrow:

..................................................................................................................
..................................................................................................................
..................................................................................................................
..................................................................................................................
..................................................................................................................

*Self-reflection is the school of wisdom.*
*— Baltasar Gracian y Morales*

# Daily Gratitude and Intention

Today I am grateful for:

.......................................................................................
.......................................................................................
.......................................................................................
.......................................................................................
.......................................................................................
.......................................................................................
.......................................................................................
.......................................................................................
.......................................................................................
.......................................................................................
.......................................................................................
.......................................................................................
.......................................................................................

Today's challenge and how it serves me to achieve my Life Priorities.

.......................................................................................
.......................................................................................
.......................................................................................
.......................................................................................
.......................................................................................

My highest Intentions for Tomorrow:

.......................................................................................
.......................................................................................
.......................................................................................
.......................................................................................
.......................................................................................

# DEC 3

*No matter what we talk about, we are talking about ourselves.*
*— Anonymous*

## Daily Gratitude and Intention

Today I am grateful for:

...........................................................................................
...........................................................................................
...........................................................................................
...........................................................................................
...........................................................................................
...........................................................................................
...........................................................................................
...........................................................................................
...........................................................................................
...........................................................................................
...........................................................................................
...........................................................................................
...........................................................................................
...........................................................................................
...........................................................................................

Today's challenge and how it serves me to achieve my Life Priorities.

...........................................................................................
...........................................................................................
...........................................................................................
...........................................................................................
...........................................................................................

My highest Intentions for Tomorrow:

...........................................................................................
...........................................................................................
...........................................................................................
...........................................................................................
...........................................................................................

*To find yourself, think for yourself. — Socrates*

## Daily Gratitude and Intention

Today I am grateful for:

.......................................................................................................
.......................................................................................................
.......................................................................................................
.......................................................................................................
.......................................................................................................
.......................................................................................................
.......................................................................................................
.......................................................................................................
.......................................................................................................
.......................................................................................................
.......................................................................................................
.......................................................................................................

Today's challenge and how it serves me to achieve my Life Priorities.

.......................................................................................................
.......................................................................................................
.......................................................................................................
.......................................................................................................
.......................................................................................................

My highest Intentions for Tomorrow:

.......................................................................................................
.......................................................................................................
.......................................................................................................
.......................................................................................................
.......................................................................................................

# DEC 5

*To believe your own thought, to believe that what is true for you in your private heart is true for all men — that is genius.*
*— Ralph Waldo Emerson*

## Daily Gratitude and Intention

Today I am grateful for:

........................................................................................
........................................................................................
........................................................................................
........................................................................................
........................................................................................
........................................................................................
........................................................................................
........................................................................................
........................................................................................
........................................................................................
........................................................................................
........................................................................................

Today's challenge and how it serves me to achieve my Life Priorities.

........................................................................................
........................................................................................
........................................................................................
........................................................................................
........................................................................................

My highest Intentions for Tomorrow:

........................................................................................
........................................................................................
........................................................................................
........................................................................................
........................................................................................

*Cherish your vision and your dreams as they are the children of your soul; the blueprints of your ultimate achievements. — Napoleon Hill*

# Daily Gratitude and Intention

Today I am grateful for:

........................................................................................................

........................................................................................................

........................................................................................................

........................................................................................................

........................................................................................................

........................................................................................................

........................................................................................................

........................................................................................................

........................................................................................................

........................................................................................................

........................................................................................................

........................................................................................................

........................................................................................................

Today's challenge and how it serves me to achieve my Life Priorities.

........................................................................................................

........................................................................................................

........................................................................................................

........................................................................................................

........................................................................................................

My highest Intentions for Tomorrow:

........................................................................................................

........................................................................................................

........................................................................................................

........................................................................................................

........................................................................................................

*If we could understand the order of the universe well enough, we would find that it surpasses all the wishes of the wisest, and that it's impossible to make it better than it is. — Leibniz*

## Daily Gratitude and Intention

Today I am grateful for:

......................................................................................................................
......................................................................................................................
......................................................................................................................
......................................................................................................................
......................................................................................................................
......................................................................................................................
......................................................................................................................
......................................................................................................................
......................................................................................................................
......................................................................................................................
......................................................................................................................
......................................................................................................................
......................................................................................................................

Today's challenge and how it serves me to achieve my Life Priorities.

......................................................................................................................
......................................................................................................................
......................................................................................................................
......................................................................................................................
......................................................................................................................

My highest Intentions for Tomorrow:

......................................................................................................................
......................................................................................................................
......................................................................................................................
......................................................................................................................
......................................................................................................................

## Daily Gratitude and Intention

Today I am grateful for:

.......................................................................................................
.......................................................................................................
.......................................................................................................
.......................................................................................................
.......................................................................................................
.......................................................................................................
.......................................................................................................
.......................................................................................................
.......................................................................................................
.......................................................................................................
.......................................................................................................
.......................................................................................................
.......................................................................................................
.......................................................................................................

Today's challenge and how it serves me to achieve my Life Priorities.

.......................................................................................................
.......................................................................................................
.......................................................................................................
.......................................................................................................
.......................................................................................................
.......................................................................................................

My highest Intentions for Tomorrow:

.......................................................................................................
.......................................................................................................
.......................................................................................................
.......................................................................................................
.......................................................................................................

# DEC 9

## Daily Gratitude and Intention

Today I am grateful for:

.................................................................................................................................
.................................................................................................................................
.................................................................................................................................
.................................................................................................................................
.................................................................................................................................
.................................................................................................................................
.................................................................................................................................
.................................................................................................................................
.................................................................................................................................
.................................................................................................................................
.................................................................................................................................
.................................................................................................................................

Today's challenge and how it serves me to achieve my Life Priorities.

.................................................................................................................................
.................................................................................................................................
.................................................................................................................................
.................................................................................................................................
.................................................................................................................................

My highest Intentions for Tomorrow:

.................................................................................................................................
.................................................................................................................................
.................................................................................................................................
.................................................................................................................................
.................................................................................................................................

*You see things and say "Why?" but I dream things that never were and I say "Why not?"*
*— George Bernard Shaw*

## Daily Gratitude and Intention

Today I am grateful for:

...........................................................................................................................................

...........................................................................................................................................

...........................................................................................................................................

...........................................................................................................................................

...........................................................................................................................................

...........................................................................................................................................

...........................................................................................................................................

...........................................................................................................................................

...........................................................................................................................................

...........................................................................................................................................

Today's challenge and how it serves me to achieve my Life Priorities.

...........................................................................................................................................

...........................................................................................................................................

...........................................................................................................................................

...........................................................................................................................................

My highest Intentions for Tomorrow:

...........................................................................................................................................

...........................................................................................................................................

...........................................................................................................................................

...........................................................................................................................................

# DEC 11

*Things don't change. We change.*
*— Henry David Thoreau*

## Daily Gratitude and Intention

Today I am grateful for:

.................................................................................
.................................................................................
.................................................................................
.................................................................................
.................................................................................
.................................................................................
.................................................................................
.................................................................................
.................................................................................
.................................................................................
.................................................................................
.................................................................................
.................................................................................

Today's challenge and how it serves me to achieve my Life Priorities.

.................................................................................
.................................................................................
.................................................................................
.................................................................................
.................................................................................

My highest Intentions for Tomorrow:

.................................................................................
.................................................................................
.................................................................................
.................................................................................
.................................................................................

## Daily Gratitude and Intention

Today I am grateful for:

.......................................................................................................
.......................................................................................................
.......................................................................................................
.......................................................................................................
.......................................................................................................
.......................................................................................................
.......................................................................................................
.......................................................................................................
.......................................................................................................
.......................................................................................................
.......................................................................................................
.......................................................................................................

Today's challenge and how it serves me to achieve my Life Priorities.

.......................................................................................................
.......................................................................................................
.......................................................................................................
.......................................................................................................
.......................................................................................................

My highest Intentions for Tomorrow:

.......................................................................................................
.......................................................................................................
.......................................................................................................
.......................................................................................................
.......................................................................................................

*Of all the attitudes we can acquire, surely the attitude of gratitude is the most important and by far the most life-changing. — Zig Ziglar*

## Daily Gratitude and Intention

Today I am grateful for:

.................................................................................
.................................................................................
.................................................................................
.................................................................................
.................................................................................
.................................................................................
.................................................................................
.................................................................................
.................................................................................
.................................................................................
.................................................................................

Today's challenge and how it serves me to achieve my Life Priorities.

.................................................................................
.................................................................................
.................................................................................
.................................................................................
.................................................................................

My highest Intentions for Tomorrow:

.................................................................................
.................................................................................
.................................................................................
.................................................................................
.................................................................................

*It is good to have an end to journey toward,
but it is the journey that matters in the end.
— Ursula K. Leguin*

## Daily Gratitude and Intention

Today I am grateful for:

........................................................................................
........................................................................................
........................................................................................
........................................................................................
........................................................................................
........................................................................................
........................................................................................
........................................................................................
........................................................................................
........................................................................................
........................................................................................
........................................................................................

Today's challenge and how it serves me to achieve my Life Priorities.

........................................................................................
........................................................................................
........................................................................................
........................................................................................
........................................................................................

My highest Intentions for Tomorrow:

........................................................................................
........................................................................................
........................................................................................
........................................................................................

# DEC 15

*Every man has his follies — and often they
are the most interesting things he has got.
— Josh Billings*

## Daily Gratitude and Intention

Today I am grateful for:

.......................................................................................................
.......................................................................................................
.......................................................................................................
.......................................................................................................
.......................................................................................................
.......................................................................................................
.......................................................................................................
.......................................................................................................
.......................................................................................................
.......................................................................................................
.......................................................................................................
.......................................................................................................

Today's challenge and how it serves me to achieve my Life Priorities.

.......................................................................................................
.......................................................................................................
.......................................................................................................
.......................................................................................................
.......................................................................................................

My highest Intentions for Tomorrow:

.......................................................................................................
.......................................................................................................
.......................................................................................................
.......................................................................................................
.......................................................................................................

## Daily Gratitude and Intention

Today I am grateful for:

..................................................................................................
..................................................................................................
..................................................................................................
..................................................................................................
..................................................................................................
..................................................................................................
..................................................................................................
..................................................................................................
..................................................................................................
..................................................................................................
..................................................................................................
..................................................................................................

Today's challenge and how it serves me to achieve my Life Priorities.

..................................................................................................
..................................................................................................
..................................................................................................
..................................................................................................
..................................................................................................

My highest Intentions for Tomorrow:

..................................................................................................
..................................................................................................
..................................................................................................
..................................................................................................
..................................................................................................

*I am open to the guidance of synchronicity,*
*and do not let expectations hinder my path.*
*— Dalai Lama*

## Daily Gratitude and Intention

Today I am grateful for:

.....................................................................................................................................
.....................................................................................................................................
.....................................................................................................................................
.....................................................................................................................................
.....................................................................................................................................
.....................................................................................................................................
.....................................................................................................................................
.....................................................................................................................................
.....................................................................................................................................
.....................................................................................................................................
.....................................................................................................................................
.....................................................................................................................................
.....................................................................................................................................

Today's challenge and how it serves me to achieve my Life Priorities.

.....................................................................................................................................
.....................................................................................................................................
.....................................................................................................................................
.....................................................................................................................................
.....................................................................................................................................

My highest Intentions for Tomorrow:

.....................................................................................................................................
.....................................................................................................................................
.....................................................................................................................................
.....................................................................................................................................
.....................................................................................................................................

*With gratitude, the entire world
suddenly becomes your friend and family.
— Dr John Demartini*

## Daily Gratitude and Intention

Today I am grateful for:

........................................................................................................

........................................................................................................

........................................................................................................

........................................................................................................

........................................................................................................

........................................................................................................

........................................................................................................

........................................................................................................

........................................................................................................

........................................................................................................

........................................................................................................

........................................................................................................

Today's challenge and how it serves me to achieve my Life Priorities.

........................................................................................................

........................................................................................................

........................................................................................................

........................................................................................................

........................................................................................................

My highest Intentions for Tomorrow:

........................................................................................................

........................................................................................................

........................................................................................................

........................................................................................................

........................................................................................................

OptimumThinking.net

# DEC 19

*Challenges are what makes life interesting;
overcoming them is what makes life meaningful.*
*— Joshua J. Marine*

## Daily Gratitude and Intention

Today I am grateful for:

.......................................................................................................
.......................................................................................................
.......................................................................................................
.......................................................................................................
.......................................................................................................
.......................................................................................................
.......................................................................................................
.......................................................................................................
.......................................................................................................
.......................................................................................................
.......................................................................................................
.......................................................................................................
.......................................................................................................
.......................................................................................................

Today's challenge and how it serves me to achieve my Life Priorities.

.......................................................................................................
.......................................................................................................
.......................................................................................................
.......................................................................................................
.......................................................................................................
.......................................................................................................

My highest Intentions for Tomorrow:

.......................................................................................................
.......................................................................................................
.......................................................................................................
.......................................................................................................
.......................................................................................................
.......................................................................................................

There are no mistakes, no coincidences. All
events are blessings given to us to learn from.
— Elizabeth Kubler-Ross

## Daily Gratitude and Intention

Today I am grateful for:

........................................................................................
........................................................................................
........................................................................................
........................................................................................
........................................................................................
........................................................................................
........................................................................................
........................................................................................
........................................................................................
........................................................................................
........................................................................................
........................................................................................
........................................................................................
........................................................................................
........................................................................................

Today's challenge and how it serves me to achieve my Life Priorities.

........................................................................................
........................................................................................
........................................................................................
........................................................................................
........................................................................................

My highest Intentions for Tomorrow:

........................................................................................
........................................................................................
........................................................................................
........................................................................................
........................................................................................

# DEC 21

## Daily Gratitude and Intention

Today I am grateful for:

......................................................................................................
......................................................................................................
......................................................................................................
......................................................................................................
......................................................................................................
......................................................................................................
......................................................................................................
......................................................................................................
......................................................................................................
......................................................................................................
......................................................................................................
......................................................................................................
......................................................................................................

Today's challenge and how it serves me to achieve my Life Priorities.

......................................................................................................
......................................................................................................
......................................................................................................
......................................................................................................
......................................................................................................

My highest Intentions for Tomorrow:

......................................................................................................
......................................................................................................
......................................................................................................
......................................................................................................
......................................................................................................

*Life is the first gift, love is the second, and understanding the third. — Margie Piercy*

# Daily Gratitude and Intention

Today I am grateful for:

..................................................................................
..................................................................................
..................................................................................
..................................................................................
..................................................................................
..................................................................................
..................................................................................
..................................................................................
..................................................................................
..................................................................................
..................................................................................
..................................................................................
..................................................................................
..................................................................................

Today's challenge and how it serves me to achieve my Life Priorities.

..................................................................................
..................................................................................
..................................................................................
..................................................................................
..................................................................................

My highest Intentions for Tomorrow:

..................................................................................
..................................................................................
..................................................................................
..................................................................................
..................................................................................

# DEC 23

*Our bodies are our gardens — our wills are our gardeners. — William Shakespeare*

## Daily Gratitude and Intention

Today I am grateful for:

...................................................................................

...................................................................................

...................................................................................

...................................................................................

...................................................................................

...................................................................................

...................................................................................

...................................................................................

...................................................................................

...................................................................................

...................................................................................

...................................................................................

...................................................................................

...................................................................................

Today's challenge and how it serves me to achieve my Life Priorities.

...................................................................................

...................................................................................

...................................................................................

...................................................................................

...................................................................................

My highest Intentions for Tomorrow:

...................................................................................

...................................................................................

...................................................................................

...................................................................................

...................................................................................

## Daily Gratitude and Intention

Today I am grateful for:

..................................................................................................
..................................................................................................
..................................................................................................
..................................................................................................
..................................................................................................
..................................................................................................
..................................................................................................
..................................................................................................
..................................................................................................
..................................................................................................
..................................................................................................
..................................................................................................

Today's challenge and how it serves me to achieve my Life Priorities.

..................................................................................................
..................................................................................................
..................................................................................................
..................................................................................................
..................................................................................................

My highest Intentions for Tomorrow:

..................................................................................................
..................................................................................................
..................................................................................................
..................................................................................................
..................................................................................................

# DEC 25

## Daily Gratitude and Intention

Today I am grateful for:

.......................................................................................
.......................................................................................
.......................................................................................
.......................................................................................
.......................................................................................
.......................................................................................
.......................................................................................
.......................................................................................
.......................................................................................
.......................................................................................
.......................................................................................
.......................................................................................

Today's challenge and how it serves me to achieve my Life Priorities.

.......................................................................................
.......................................................................................
.......................................................................................
.......................................................................................
.......................................................................................

My highest Intentions for Tomorrow:

.......................................................................................
.......................................................................................
.......................................................................................
.......................................................................................
.......................................................................................

*Learning the game of power requires a certain way of looking at the world, a shifting of perspective.*
*— Robert Greene*

# DEC 26

## Daily Gratitude and Intention

Today I am grateful for:

........................................................................................

........................................................................................

........................................................................................

........................................................................................

........................................................................................

........................................................................................

........................................................................................

........................................................................................

........................................................................................

........................................................................................

........................................................................................

........................................................................................

Today's challenge and how it serves me to achieve my Life Priorities.

........................................................................................

........................................................................................

........................................................................................

........................................................................................

........................................................................................

My highest Intentions for Tomorrow:

........................................................................................

........................................................................................

........................................................................................

........................................................................................

........................................................................................

# DEC 27

## Daily Gratitude and Intention

Today I am grateful for:

........................................................................................................

........................................................................................................

........................................................................................................

........................................................................................................

........................................................................................................

........................................................................................................

........................................................................................................

........................................................................................................

........................................................................................................

........................................................................................................

........................................................................................................

Today's challenge and how it serves me to achieve my Life Priorities.

........................................................................................................

........................................................................................................

........................................................................................................

........................................................................................................

My highest Intentions for Tomorrow:

........................................................................................................

........................................................................................................

........................................................................................................

........................................................................................................

........................................................................................................

## Daily Gratitude and Intention

Today I am grateful for:

..............................................................................................................
..............................................................................................................
..............................................................................................................
..............................................................................................................
..............................................................................................................
..............................................................................................................
..............................................................................................................
..............................................................................................................
..............................................................................................................
..............................................................................................................
..............................................................................................................
..............................................................................................................

Today's challenge and how it serves me to achieve my Life Priorities.

..............................................................................................................
..............................................................................................................
..............................................................................................................
..............................................................................................................
..............................................................................................................

My highest Intentions for Tomorrow:

..............................................................................................................
..............................................................................................................
..............................................................................................................
..............................................................................................................
..............................................................................................................

# DEC 29

*There are plenty of good ideas, if only they can be backed with power and brought into reality.*
*— Winston Churchill*

## Daily Gratitude and Intention

Today I am grateful for:

........................................................................................................

........................................................................................................

........................................................................................................

........................................................................................................

........................................................................................................

........................................................................................................

........................................................................................................

........................................................................................................

........................................................................................................

........................................................................................................

........................................................................................................

........................................................................................................

........................................................................................................

Today's challenge and how it serves me to achieve my Life Priorities.

........................................................................................................

........................................................................................................

........................................................................................................

........................................................................................................

........................................................................................................

My highest Intentions for Tomorrow:

........................................................................................................

........................................................................................................

........................................................................................................

........................................................................................................

........................................................................................................

## Daily Gratitude and Intention

Today I am grateful for:

........................................................................................
........................................................................................
........................................................................................
........................................................................................
........................................................................................
........................................................................................
........................................................................................
........................................................................................
........................................................................................
........................................................................................
........................................................................................
........................................................................................
........................................................................................

Today's challenge and how it serves me to achieve my Life Priorities.

........................................................................................
........................................................................................
........................................................................................
........................................................................................
........................................................................................

My highest Intentions for Tomorrow:

........................................................................................
........................................................................................
........................................................................................
........................................................................................
........................................................................................

# DEC 31

*We do not see things as they are; we see things as we are. — The Talmud*

## Daily Gratitude and Intention

Today I am grateful for:

........................................................................................................................................
........................................................................................................................................
........................................................................................................................................
........................................................................................................................................
........................................................................................................................................
........................................................................................................................................
........................................................................................................................................
........................................................................................................................................
........................................................................................................................................
........................................................................................................................................
........................................................................................................................................
........................................................................................................................................

Today's challenge and how it serves me to achieve my Life Priorities.

........................................................................................................................................
........................................................................................................................................
........................................................................................................................................
........................................................................................................................................
........................................................................................................................................

My highest Intentions for Tomorrow:

........................................................................................................................................
........................................................................................................................................
........................................................................................................................................
........................................................................................................................................
........................................................................................................................................

# A Work in Progress

Life is a work in progress and so is this journal. Please

contact us if you have any suggestions as to how to

improve it or quotes you think should be added in the

next edition. Simply email info@OptimumThinking.net

You can also join our mailing list to receive updates when

new editions are available. Simply fill in the form on

www.optimumthinking.net/InspiredLifeJournal

We look forward to receiving your feedback

and suggestions.

Made in the USA
Columbia, SC
08 February 2018